The German Shorthaired Pointer

The German Shorthaired Pointer:

A hunter's guide to the selection, care, training, and handling of America's most popular pointing breed.

By

David Gowdey

Wide Sky Press
New Orleans and Flagstaff

Wide Sky Press
207 Country Club Blvd
Slidell, LA 70458
www.wideskypress.com

ISBN-13: 978-0-9822330-0-9
ISBN-10: 0-9822330-0-0

Library of Congress Cataloging in Publication Data
1. The German Shorthaired Pointer.
2. Upland game bird shooting-United States.

Contents

This book is dedicated to the family and friends without whose support, in so many ways, this book would never have come to fruition.

It is also dedicated to those generations of von Geldie Shorthairs that have so enriched my life. Annchen, the mother of my line, Rosie and Greta, and Billy the best of them all.

Foreword

The author with two generations of his vonGeldie German Shorthairs: Rosie, Annchen, and Billy.

Anyone who has owned a traditional German Shorthaired pointer will tell you that there is something special about the breed. German Shorthairs are a unique mix of extraordinary hunting abilities, keen intelligence, endearing and occasionally exasperating personality traits, deep loyalty and affection, physical beauty and toughness, and tolerance for human foibles and particularly the foibles of small children.

One of the trends in modern dog breed books is to play up the positive aspects of the breed while downplaying the negatives in order to portray the breed as the perfect pet for everybody. This book will buck that trend. While the German Shorthair is the ideal breed for many owners, they are not the perfect breed for everyone. German Shorthairs are a hunting breed in fact as well as name –and non-hunters should think twice about whether they would do justice to the dog they might get. Like most pointing breeds, German Shorthairs require lots of open space in which to run regularly. On a typical hunt, a German Shorthair will run more than 30 miles during the course of the day. A half hour walk each day is not enough exercise to keep the breed out of mischief. They need to run – and urban dwellers who do not have a place for them to run should consider another breed.

German Shorthairs are sociable dogs that don't do well isolated from human contact. Unlike many other hunting breeds, traditional German Shorthairs don't do well spending all of their time in an outdoor kennel. I firmly believe that German Shorthairs do best as an indoor dog – living life as part of a social unit. If you want a breed that will primarily be an outside dog – you are better off looking at a breed with more independence such as a Pointer. On the other hand, if your situation is such that you can offer a German Shorthair your love and companionship as well as plenty of time spent afield – you are likely to have found the perfect canine companion.

Under normal circumstances, German Shorthairs are vivacious, friendly, affectionate dogs with their owners and family. With strangers and other dogs, they are often somewhat aloof until they know them better. Even when they do know and like other people, their true loyalties will always lay with their owner and family.

Shorthairs are extremely intelligent and playful –which can sometimes lead to mischief. They have a knack for getting into places they shouldn't, and doing things you don't want them to do. For a number of years I had a running battle with one of my Shorthair bitches – a liver cutie named Rosie. Every spring I would try to plant rose bushes to liven up my back yard. I would put fencing around the plants, repellant around the roots, and use whatever tricks I could think of. Within three days she would have figured a way around the obstacles and would have uprooted the plants. She thought this was a great game – but it was too much for my pocket book. The back yard remained devoid of rose bushes.

With people they like, German Shorthairs have such a friendly and affectionate disposition that it is easy to see them as simply lovers and schmoozers. That is only part of the picture. They are also very tough dogs and that toughness should not be taken lightly. Beneath those jowls, German Shorthairs have a set of teeth that are still designed for killing. They are formidable weapons. I have seen my German Shorthairs kill coyotes, and know others that run in packs that hunt mountain lions. It is common for German Shorthairs to kill small animals – including cats if they are not trained otherwise. They are also decent watchdogs. Though not particularly aggressive toward humans, when protecting their

"Keeping a German Shorthair strictly as a pet –without letting them hunt as they were bred to do – is like keeping a Mozart from ever playing a musical instrument or writing a note."

owners, or children, German Shorthairs can be ferocious – and inflict serious harm on intruders. Moreover, while German Shorthairs don't typically tend to start fights with other dogs – as the saying goes they generally finish them.

As a hobby breeder, I don't choose to sell my pups to non-hunters or those who intend to raise the dogs as purely outside dogs. I'm not nasty about this, or confrontational. I just personally don't believe that these situations are a suitable fit for the breed. I have been criticized by friends who are non-hunters for this policy – they argue that a German Shorthair can live a perfectly happy life in a non-hunting household. In the past I've had trouble enunciating why I don't really believe this, why I think that it's important that German Shorthairs be allowed to do those functions for which they were bred. I've finally come up with an analogy that may explain the issue as I see it. In my mind, keeping a German Shorthair strictly as a pet –without letting them hunt as they were bred to do – is like keeping a Mozart, who could hear the melodies in his mind, from ever playing a musical instrument or writing a note.

Could either be truly happy not being allowed to use the remarkable talent with which they were born and which is a source of so much joy? In even the most loving household – wouldn't there always be something missing? I believe so – which is why I have the policy I do.

I used to joke that I was raised by a pack of German Shorthairs, but the truth is that statement isn't too far off of the mark. There has been one or more (generally more) German Shorthairs in my home for nearly forty years now. If I add to those the puppies that started out with us, the Shorthairs owned by good friends who often joined us in the field, the Shorthairs that I helped others train, and those that I've seen in competition or in the kennels of other breeders – well, I've seen a lot of German Shorthairs in my time. I am grateful for the privilege. This great breed of dogs has enriched my life, filling it with unconditional love and joy, and taught me much about life, the natural world, and my place in the universe. They say that owners come to resemble their dog breed of choice – I hope that's true. I can't think of a higher complement.

Since Bede Maxwell wrote her magnificent "the New Complete German Shorthaired Pointer" most German Shorthair books in the United States in recent years have been written from the perspective of people who show or field trial their dogs. While I have no problem with those who field trial or show their dogs, I do believe that their perspective is often substantially different in many respects from the perspective of the hunter who wants a German Shorthair as a foot hunting partner and household companion. The characteristics and attributes horseback field trialers, and to a lesser extent show competitors, look for in their German Shorthairs are often quite different from those that would best serve a hunter. Yet over this same period, the traditional German Shorthair has become the favorite upland dog of the American hunter. It seemed, therefore, that there was a need for a new book on the German Shorthair written for the hunter by someone who has spent decades hunting, breeding, training, and living with generations of Shorthairs rather than competing them or making a profession of training dogs.

This is why I have written this book from the perspective of someone whose German Shorthairs are primarily hunting partners and family companions – as those old Germans who developed the breed envisioned. Over three decades and a bit I have walked thousands of miles in the uplands with German Shorthairs, hunting dozens of different game species on three continents. I have also spent hundreds of days in duck blinds with German Shorthairs who retrieved those ducks and geese that I was fortunate enough to drop. I consider myself blessed in having been able to spend such time in the field with this wonderful breed – and this book is my attempt to pass on some of the knowledge and wisdom I have gained about German Shorthairs over the years. In doing so, I have tried to give the hunter honest information that will help them find and train a German Shorthair that will be a fine hunting partner and loyal friend for the span of its days.

As a hunter and lover of the breed, one of the trends that I have found most painful over the last two decades has been the steady increase in the number of German Shorthairs that wind up in animal shelters (hopefully to be rescued). Thirty years ago one rarely saw a German Shorthair in the pound. Today it is not uncommon. There are certainly a number of these dogs who wind up in the pound because they had the misfortune to be purchased by irresponsible, and sometimes abusive, owners. However, my impressions have been that the number of German Shorthairs arriving in animal shelters because of hyperactivity, lack of hunting and retrieving instincts, and temperament problems has been increasing at an alarming rate. Many new hunters have told me that the German Shorthairs they or their friends have purchased have not matched the descriptions of the breed they read in books and magazines.

I believe that this has happened because too many breeders have moved away from breeding German Shorthairs primarily for hunters, and instead are focused on breeding dogs upon which they can hang competitive titles. I hope this book will help new hunters find and train hunting German Shorthairs that are ideal for their needs –and avoid those puppies whose un-Shorthair like characteristics might ultimately cause them to wind up in the pound.

The opinions and criticisms I have put in these pages are based upon first hand observation and knowledge that I have gathered over nearly forty years with the breed. They are mine alone – and I take full responsibility for these opinions. I have not come to them lightly. There are field trialers in particular who will object to some of the criticism and opinions contained in this book. They are certainly entitled to their opinions – and will find other books written by field trial judges and breeders that will be more sympathetic to their perspective.

1

Introduction

The first German Shorthair I ever laid eyes upon was Gretel, who my uncle Charles DeMenna first brought from California to Arizona in 1968. She was a beautiful three year old with a ticked body and liver head who was a wonderful introduction to the breed. She was tough as nails, a skilled retriever, an expert Pointer with a good nose, and she had enough personality to fill Carnegie hall. As I look back over forty years, her non-hunting exploits stick in my mind as much as her exploits in the field.

Like the time she was staying in the garage, where my uncle had set up her whelping box, waiting to give birth to a litter of pups that were due any day. At some point during the night she managed to open a chuck box with camping supplies that was stored in the garage. The next morning when they checked on her, her face was covered in some unidentifiable white powder – which alarmed everyone until it was determined that she had eaten an entire large box of Bisquick baking mix – cardboard and all. It didn't disturb her iron constitution a bit, though I remained moderately hopeful for a short period that she would be pooping pancakes. She gave birth to a fine healthy litter two days later. In short, she was a German Shorthair through and through.

At that time, the conventional wisdom was that Gambel's quail, the most common quail in my home state of Arizona, couldn't be hunted with a pointing dog. The books said that their trickiness and propensity to run would ruin a good pointing dog, and that the hot, dry conditions and rugged terrain were simply too rough for a pointing dog. Gretel proved to many doubters that, in fact, German Shorthairs were almost ideally suited to hunting Gambel's quail – and that in reality, Gambel's quail hunted over good German Shorthairs could provide some of the greatest sport in the world. This is now widely recognized, but in the late 1960s and 1970s – this was close to heresy.

The reason that conventional wisdom had deemed Arizona a wasteland for quail hunting, and Gambel's quail a pariah game bird where pointing dogs were concerned, has an interesting story attached. It is a story that also helps explain how German Shorthairs became the most popular pointing breed in the United States.

In the early years of the 20th century, Arizona was viewed as something of a hunter's Shangri-la. It was the last frontier in the lower 46 states – so wild that it had not even qualified for statehood. Game of every sort abounded – from enormous mule deer and desert bighorn sheep, to Merriam's turkey, to quail coveys that were reputed to number in the millions. It was a favorite stomping ground for men like Theodore Roosevelt, Zane Grey, and Aldo Leopold – all of whom wrote about their experiences in the Arizona territory. Their accounts, in turn, inspired some very wealthy and influential sportsmen to visit Arizona to check out these new quail. These men and women loaded their blooded walking horses, their finest field trial Pointers and Setters, and an army of servants and handlers onto specially chartered trains and headed for the Arizona territory.

According to old-timers in a position to know, these gentile expeditions proved to be disasters. Even though quail abounded, the fast moving, big running Pointers and Setters they brought with them had great difficulty scenting birds in the hot, dry conditions. They suffered from the cactus and tore their pads on the rough lava rock. The range at which they worked, a quarter mile or more, often put them out of sight and made them difficult to locate when they went on point in the rugged country. On top of that, the quail themselves drove the dogs crazy. Gambel's quail would run out from under point after a few minutes – which meant that hunters who took a while to find a dog on point would often arrive to see quail running away and a frustrated dog breaking point and chasing the birds until they flushed.

Rather than recognizing that Gambel's quail were quite different from the eastern Bobwhite, and that the tactics and dog characteristics suited for Bobwhite weren't very effective on Gambel's quail – these influential sportsmen blamed the birds and the conditions for the poor sport. This, in turn, became the conventional wisdom for nearly three quarters of a century.

That isn't to say that nobody hunted quail in Arizona with a pointing dog during the first half of the twentieth century. There were always some Arizona sportsmen who hunted desert quail with a pointing dog with varying degrees of success. In *A Sand County Almanac*, Aldo Leopold writes of hunting Gambel's quail in Arizona with a little English Setter in the 1920s. However, the truth is that the two breeds that dominated the American uplands for most of the first two thirds of the twentieth century, Pointers and English Setters, were not ideal dogs with which to hunt Gambel's quail

Field trialers and plantation hunting sportsmen had to a large extent turned these breeds into fast moving, far ranging dogs that, while they may have been deadly on bobwhite under the right conditions, weren't well suited to hunting desert quail. Not only did their fast pace and exclusive reliance on air scent (which often doesn't carry well on hot, dry air) make them tend to outrun their noses in desert conditions, but their lack of natural retrieving instinct was a liability in hunting tough birds that were capable of absorbing a lot of shot and still running for cover. With bird numbers so abundant that a foot hunter could expect good sport even without a dog – hunters just didn't see the need for dogs whose weaknesses in the hunting field were often as prominent as their strengths.

Nevertheless, many hunters who loved the idea of following a pointing dog in Arizona, if not always the reality, kept searching for dogs that could handle desert quail. In the 1950s, the Weimeraner became a "fad" among American hunters – and a number of Arizona hunters thought that might be the magic breed. Widely touted as the wonder dog that could do everything from track an elk to point and retrieve a limit of quail, in the late 1950s and early 1960s a number of hunters brought the breed to Arizona and tried them for hunting desert quail. (Arizona lore says that it was the German air force pilots who came to train at Luke Air Force base who first brought Weimeraners to the state – but I can't find any hard information to substantiate this story.)

German Shorthairs hunting Gambel's quail in Arizona.

What these hunters found was that the working style of the continental dogs such as the Weimeraner was much better suited to desert hunting than the working style of the big running Pointers and Setters. They found that under optimal conditions very good sport could be had hunting Gambel's quail over their dogs. However, the Weimeraner's average nose and relatively weak bird hunting instincts still made them less than ideal for hunting desert quail. On the many days when scenting conditions were difficult the average Weimeraner couldn't find the birds.

It wasn't until German Shorthairs such as Gretel began showing up around this time that Arizona hunters realized that they had finally found an almost perfect breed for Gambel's quail hunting. The German Shorthair's outstanding nose, moderate range and pace, strong hunting instincts, rugged toughness, keen intelligence, and good retrieving skills proved the perfect match for both the birds and the terrain and conditions in Arizona. As a consequence, by the mid 1970s quail hunting over pointing dogs began to take off in the state and continues to grow in popularity to this day.

I knew a fair number of Arizona hunters who bought and hunted Weimeraners in the 1960s – the vast majority of them switched to German Shorthairs once they were able to retire their Weimeraners. They recognized the weaknesses that the Weimeraners had where desert hunting was concerned, and that the German Shorthair as a breed had strengths that the Weimeraner lacked. The German Shorthairs won these hunters over by their performance in the field rather than hype or breed promotion – a pattern that was repeated over the years in different regions on different game birds all around the US.

The German Shorthair was first created to be a versatile hunting dog for the German middle class hunter. This hunter didn't have access to the great estates of the nobility with their abundant game. Instead he had to hunt local farms and wasteland along with many others. He needed a dog whose nose wouldn't miss much, and who would help him find and take what game was available – from partridge to duck, hare to stag. In response to these needs the Germans developed a pointing dog with an outstanding nose and the ability to use both air scent and ground scent to track game. They gave the breed a love of water and retrieving, and the courage to tackle dangerous game and vermin. They made it a moderate ranged dog that hunted for the gun, and gave it a moderate pace that enabled it to hunt all day in a variety of conditions. They also made it a biddable, intelligent, family companion for middle class houses that had neither the income nor space for large kennels or more than a couple of dogs. These same characteristics have made the Shorthair the supreme "meat dog" – a dog that fills the game bag under even the worst conditions.

It is ironic, but the same characteristics that made the German Shorthair such an effective hunter were ridiculed by the American sporting dog establishment. "Meat dog" was used as a pejorative – as though the dog that put the most game in the bag was somehow the lesser dog. Even more ironic is the fact that this ridicule was happening at the same time that the GSP was rapidly becoming a favorite of American bird hunters and supplanting the Pointers and Setters that were the favorites of the establishment.

The German Shorthair has a well earned reputation as a "meat dog" that puts game in the bag.

For nearly a century the "class" bird dogs in America had been bred first and foremost to hunt bobwhite quail. Bobwhites were the most widespread gallinaceous game bird in America well into the early 1960s, with huntable populations found from Massachusetts to New Mexico. The Bobwhite was, and remains, beloved by hunters for a number of reasons. It is normally found in relatively open grassland and edge habitat that is easy for dogs to hunt, and in climates that generally provide excellent scenting conditions. It gathers in coveys, which put out a large amount of scent, and when located these coveys hold well under point. The dogs they developed to hunt these birds tended to run so fast and range so widely that they were difficult to follow on foot. On the great plantations of the South, they were often followed on horseback or by wagons or vehicles – and hunters only disembarked when dogs were spotted on point.

In the decades following World War II, American bird hunting changed profoundly. For more than a half century, Americans had been moving from the farm to the cities and suburbs. Suburbs began to sprawl into rural areas - turning millions of acres of farmland, grassland, forest and marsh into subdivisions and shopping malls. Habitat was fragmented by an ever-increasing network of roads, highways, and freeways. Fewer farmers were forced to produce more food -which in turn led to radical changes in both land ownership patterns and farming itself. In their quest to get greater returns per acre, farming became more mechanized and dependent upon chemical fertilizers and pesticides – with obvious adverse affects upon wildlife populations. In addition, a century of economic over-exploitation of America's public lands and

12

waters resulted in widespread deforestation, overgrazing, pollution, and the destruction of wetlands, which left diminishing wildlife populations – a good portion of which was struggling to survive in degraded habitat. The range of the bobwhite began to contract dramatically – a contraction that still continues today. Bobwhites were extirpated over a substantial portion of their former range, and populations in many areas that used to boast abundant populations of bobwhite crashed. At the same time, a good portion of the US population began to move west – and got to know and value the western quail species. Moreover, new game birds had been introduced and thrived in areas that had seen native species such as prairie grouse disappear.

These other species posed challenges for dogs that "Gentleman Bob" rarely matched. Chukar and the western quail species are found in rugged terrain, where scenting conditions are often difficult – and they have a propensity to run rather than hold tight. This propensity is also shared by that other immigrant - the Ring-necked Pheasant. As a consequence, many American hunters soon found that the big ranging Pointers and Setters were not really well suited to the type of hunting they were actually doing. Other hunters became more eclectic in the game they pursued, often hunting more than one upland bird species as well as waterfowl during the course of a season. A breed of hunting dog that could handle waterfowl as well as upland game was quite attractive. For these hunters, the characteristics of the GSP soon came to be recognized as better fitting the hunting they were doing than those of the "class" bird dogs favored by the "establishment."

Yet, at a time when American hunters were learning to value the hunting qualities of the GSP – it's moderate range and pace, its excellent scenting powers, it's strong natural pointing and retrieving instincts, and its calm disposition and intelligent bidability – many American bird dog writers were still stuck in the past. As late as the 1980s the breed was still being criticized in books for being a plodder because it didn't range as far and fast as the Pointers and Setters –even though this made it a more effective hunter. It was criticized for not being as stylish on point because it often pointed with its head where

German Shorthairs are handsome and intense on point –contrary to the claims of some American hunting dog writers. Photo by Margaret Cotton.

the scent was strongest instead of always being held aloft. It was criticized for being too willing to hunt with its nose down – even though that may be the only place to find scent left by running birds in dry conditions. It was unjustly criticized for lacking fire and intensity because of its cooperative nature and easy trainability. All of these criticisms were demonstrably wrong or irrelevant where hunting was concerned – but they were reported in print nonetheless. Not surprisingly, the writers that were most critical of the traditional German Shorthairs were almost exclusively those with strong roots in the field trial establishment rather than those who were first and foremost hunters.

Despite this criticism in the hunting press – American hunters, relying on first hand experience and word of mouth, began moving to the breed in increasing numbers in the 1960s and 1970s. By the 1980s the German Shorthair was the breed most commonly used on game preserves and plantations – where finding, pointing and retrieving birds was a matter of financial necessity. It became a favorite breed of hunting guides as well. By the late 1990s, the German Shorthair was by registration, the most popular breed of pointing dog in the United States – finally surpassing the Setters and Pointers. Interestingly, the rise of the Brittany, another continental breed, paralleled that of the GSP – though not in the same numbers. By the 1990s, the Brittany was also well established in the "Big Four" most popular pointing breeds in the US.

Unfortunately, the misguided criticisms of the field trialers and their spokespersons in the bird dog establishment – while they didn't affect the breed's growing popularity with hunters - were to have an adverse affect on the German Shorthair. In the 1960s and 1970s a small group of horseback field trial breeders, many of whom had been former Pointer breeders and trialers, began turning out "souped up" German Shorthairs. Breeders like Hjalmer Olsen, Dean Kerl and others began producing fireball Shorthairs with strong Pointer characteristics that worked in a manner more consistent with the old Pointers and Setters than the traditional GSP. Lines such as Moesgaard became well known for dogs that not only worked like Pointers, they even looked more like Pointers than GSPs – and there were widespread allegations of commonplace crossbreeding with Pointers. While such allegations were almost impossible to prove (until DNA testing became possible a few years ago), many experienced GSP owners believe that crossbreeding to Pointers became so widespread among field trialers that many strains of field trial GSPs became genetically little more than hybrid Pointers. I share that belief. Essentially, these field trialers split the breed – and this split has gotten progressively more pronounced in the years since. Many breeders of traditional GSPs now try not to breed to field trial strains because they believe such strains have little to offer except a big run – at a very high cost in terms of losing other Shorthair characteristics.

To an outsider to the world of pointing dogs, or a novice to the world of field trials all of this might seem a bit confusing. If the GSP was proving itself superior in the hunting field, why try and alter it to be more like the big running Pointers and

Setters it was replacing? Well, there are two main reasons:

The first is that the breed clubs for the German Shorthair refused to develop a field trial format appropriate for the breed. Instead, they simply adopted the standard field trial formats of the AKC and the American Field (FDSB) organizations – formats designed specifically for Pointers and Setters. In these formats, big running dogs are followed on horseback – and dogs are judged primarily on their speed and range rather than their bird finding ability or retrieving skills.

This has affected their hunting characteristics. In scientific surveys conducted in the early years of this decade at the National Championship field trials held at the Ames plantation each year it was shown that the best field trial Pointers in the country were finding and pointing only 5% of the available radio collared birds. Similar studies on experienced hunting Pointers showed that they routinely found an average of 35% of available birds.

By permitting GSP field trials to be run on horseback rather than on foot, strong competitive pressure was generated to turn this foot-hunting breed into a big running breed that justified the use of horses to follow them. Over the years, this encouraged breeders and handlers that wanted to win to produce ever faster, bigger running dogs – until their dogs are now often closer in conformation and working characteristics to those field trial style Pointers rather than the traditional hunting GSP.

The second is that there was a small group of experienced hunters who had grown up for generations hunting over Pointers and Setters and who had trouble accepting that their previous notions of what constituted a "class" bird dog were outdated. Their prejudices were reinforced by those outdoor writers who shared them, and who criticized the GSP for the very characteristics that arguably made it a superior hunting dog.

Moreover, to get the best results from a GSP in the hunting field requires that it be hunted in a manner fundamentally different from the way that many American hunters were used to hunting their Pointers and Setters. GSPs produce best when they work cooperatively as partners with the hunter – hunting as a team. Many American bird hunters, used to highly independent Pointers and   Setters, were simply used to following their dogs with little cooperative interaction. Such hunters were more comfortable hunting with dogs that had the independence of Pointers – and were therefore supportive of the efforts of horseback field trialers to produce GSPs that were more Pointer-like.

The end result has been that for the past twenty-five years there has been a growing split in the breed between the field trial strains and the traditional hunting strains that has gotten so pronounced that some hunters have given up on American German Shorthairs altogether. These hunters have taken to importing German strains, which they identify by their German name – Deutsch Kurzhaars (DKs). They keep their registration separate from the American German Shorthairs and refuse to register any pups from DK/American GSP matings. They do this because they believe that the influences of the field trialers and those who want to make the American GSP more like a Pointer – have significantly degraded the characteristics that made the GSP the most popular versatile/pointing breed in the world among hunters.

Other hunters have gravitated toward the testing regime of the North American Versatile Hunting Dog Association (NAVHDA) –which implements tests patterned on those used by the Germans to assess the hunting abilities and quality of their German Shorthairs. The German Shorthair is the most popular breed in NAVHDA, which has become a stronghold of those who value the traditional versatility of the breed. To a large extent NAVHDA has taken over as the center of the traditional GSP world in the United States – supplanting the breed clubs that have come to be dominated by field trial and show competitors.

While I believe that the criticism of those who say that the field trialers and their supporters have done harm to the GSP as a hunting breed is amply justified – I still believe that there are plenty of hunters and breeders in the US breeding traditional German Shorthairs that are as good as any in the world. However, as younger hunters increasingly encounter "German Shorthairs" that are too hyperactive to be comfortable family members, that lack strong natural pointing and retrieving instincts, that dislike water, whose independence makes them difficult to train and handle, and whose fast pace and big range make them difficult to handle in the field – it remains questionable whether these "improved" American strains will continue to perform well enough in the field to maintain the GSP's place as the favorite pointing breed of American hunters.

This brings up the question of what is a "traditional" German Shorthair. This is best answered by briefly discussing the characteristics of a good traditional German Shorthair. Just as horseback field trialers are looking for specific characteristics of run and range in their dogs, so too hunters look for specific characteristics in their dogs. The German Shorthair, as will be discussed in further detail in the next chapter, was developed first and foremost as a hunting companion for a hunter on foot. As such, a traditional GSP is a cooperative, social dog who is most comfortable hunting as a team with the hunter. This cooperative nature in turn makes the GSP easy to train, and a good family companion. The traditional GSP also has strong natural pointing and retrieving instincts, and many of them naturally honor the point of other dogs. They are also natural water dogs with a love of swimming and retrieving from water. Traditional German Shorthairs work at a moderate range and pace that allows them to stay in contact with their hunters and hunt for the gun all day. Hunters typically don't have to run after them to stay in contact, or worry about them running off and self-hunting. They also are well known for the quality of their noses – choke bore is a description often used – which often enables them to find game where other breeds fail. Finally, they are a medium sized dog with physical characteristics that make them ideal for upland hunting in moderate sized fields and broken country, as well as warmer weather waterfowl hunting. The breed standard, fortunately, still enshrines those physical characteristics.

Flick, a New Zealand German Shorthair owned by Margaret Cotton, shows the traditional German Shorthair's love of water. In the USA, the German Shorthair is struggling to retain its traditional versatile characteristics. Photo by the owner.

This book is written for owners of traditional German Shorthairs, those hunters who wish to own a GSP, and particularly those owners who hunt their German Shorthairs. The training methods and hunting tips in this book were tested on, and developed for, traditional GSPs. The stories contained here are stories about traditional hunting Shorthairs. I hope that they prove useful and that you enjoy this book as much as I enjoyed writing it.

2

The Origins of the German Shorthair

To understand the development of the German Shorthaired pointer, it's important to understand the cultural and historic forces that led to its creation. Prior to the Napoleonic wars, what we now know as Germany was actually a collection of independent states governed by a variety of kings, princes, dukes and other aristocrats. As elsewhere in Europe, hunting was primarily the sport of the nobility and wealthy landowners who could afford to keep large kennels of dogs. Because they could afford to house and feed large numbers of dogs, these landowners typically had a wide variety of specialized breeds to hunt different types of game. They had tracking hounds for big game, coursing hounds for foxes and hares, breeds to control vermin, retrievers for hunting waterfowl, and Pointers and Setters for hunting upland game.

The defeat and occupation of these states by the revolutionary French soldiers of Napoleon caused a political revolution. The aristocracy was stripped of many of its privileges and much of the land was seized and divided up among peasants – creating a new middle class. This new German middle class was given many of the privileges that had previously been limited to the nobility – including hunting. In the process, a new German nationalism was created – where people began to think of themselves as German rather than simply citizens of a particular principality or duchy. At least in part the wars also generated a resentment of the nobility, who were blamed for ineffective leadership that led to Germany being used, insulted, and abused by a succession of great European powers.

After the fall of Napoleon, the efforts of the aristocracy to reestablish the old order were met by strong resistance from the new middle class – and the four decades after Waterloo were periods of revolution and political turmoil in much of

CH Baretta vom Otterbach MH,NAI, UTII, D1, AZP1,HN, SG. A German bred
Shorthair owned by Cindy Stahle that is a fine example of the modern Deutsch
Kurzhaar

Germany. Prussia and Austria vied for preeminence in the new
Germany that was emerging – each contributing inadvertently
to strengthening the new middle class as they pursued their
various political agendas. Out of this turmoil, as a result of a
strong new spirit of German nationalism, a new, united,
modern Germany emerged under the leadership of the
Prussian King.

The whole nation was seized with this sense of nationalism
and the desire to make the new Germany a great state that was
at least the equal of the other great European powers such as
France and Great Britain. This rivalry and feeling of patriotism
trickled down throughout the whole society to the most

mundane activities. German citizens wanted German products and they wanted them to be superior to the English, Russian and French equivalents. Patriotic Germans not only wanted Germany to be recognized as a great power second to none – they wanted things German to be recognized in the same manner. Their efforts produced results – by the middle of the century German industry and technology was second to none and Germany had become a truly great European power. The effort to create a great German foot-hunting dog was just a small manifestation of this greater national mindset.

1870 is a notable year for a number of reasons. In European history, it is the year that the newly united Germany went to war with, and defeated, France – the greatest land power in Europe. It is also the year that a group of German hunters and dog breeders got together to create a studbook for a new German pointing breed that would be, in their opinion, superior to the French Braques and the English Pointers and Setters that were the standard of excellence for European upland dogs at the time.

For patriotic reasons, they used as their starting point the old German Pointer. The German Pointer was typical of those regional breeds developed from the Spanish Pointer in the 18th and early 19th centuries. Pictures of the German Pointer show a hound like, stocky dog somewhat similar in shape and coloration to the current Bracco Italiano. Like the dog breeders in other countries, the Germans had crossed the Spanish Pointer with the famous St. Hubert's hounds and a variety of native tracking hound breeds to improve its scenting ability, its ability to handle fur as well as birds, and its temperament. The exact mix of hound breeds involved is lost to history. German sources say that the breed was crossed with scent hounds – which has at various times been translated as bloodhounds. While the Germans steadfastly deny that they used the breed that the English call the bloodhound in creating the German Pointer, the scent hounds they used would have worked in a similar manner – with a tendency to keep their nose down and to focus on ground scent. The mix that they arrived at was reportedly a slower paced, close working dog that had a hound like temperament and toughness. Like the Bracco Italiano it

The Germans wanted a hunting dog that was more than just a pointer. Here Flick, a New Zealand Shorthair owned by Margaret Cotton, shows the enthusiasm for water for which the breed is noted.

was a close working dog that thoroughly covered the ground near the hunter.

However, as an upland hunting dog it was outclassed by the French and British pointing breeds of the time. Its limited use of air scent and its stocky, short-coupled build curtailed both its speed and range. Accounts also seem to indicate that some strains had weak scenting powers. Next to the French Braques and the English Setters and Pointers it would have looked like a plodding carthorse compared to thoroughbreds.

After some deliberation, the Germans decided that they didn't want to just get the breed's nose up and increase its range and pace so that it would be a worthy competitor for the French and British bird dogs– they wanted this new dog to do even more. They wanted it to surpass the French and British dogs as a hunting dog. They wanted it to be the ultimate foot hunter's dog. In addition to the flashy work on upland birds that the French and British dogs showed, they wanted the breed to be a strong retriever from land and water, they wanted it to be able to track big game and deal with predators, and they wanted it to be easy for a novice to train and keep inside of a house. It should be the kind of dog that a middle class hunter, who could only have one dog, would dream of – and they wanted to add these improvements while also keeping the strong points of the old German Pointer. With Teutonic thoroughness, they outlined their idea of the ideal dog for a foot hunter, and then set about creating it. History shows that they achieved remarkable success.

At first many of the breeders believed that the best way to accomplish their objectives was to experiment with crossbreeds while keeping the conformation of the old German Pointer. These breeders were led by Karl Brandt. They placed excessive emphasis on traditional German characteristics like the roundness of the ears, and head shape. For the first decade of the Club, this faction held sway and limited registration in the studbook to dogs that had the old German conformation. Unfortunately, trying to create a superior hunting dog while limiting it to the stocky structure of the old German Pointer was a recipe for disaster. This was like trying to make a Grand Prix winner by putting a racecar engine in a milk wagon. It simply didn't work. One of the most famous German hunting dog experts of the time, Prince Albrecht zu Solms-Braunfeld, advised his colleagues to forget their slavish devotion to the old conformation. He essentially advised them that form followed function, and if they concentrated on breeding to meet the functions they desired then the form would sort itself out. His advice was to breed best to best based upon performance in the field. This was sage advice, and fortunately, after more than a decade of slow progress the group took the advice to heart. They changed the rules of the studbook to allow breeding the best performers to the best performers. From that point forward the development of the breed would proceed quickly.

The exact mix of dogs that went into those early German Shorthairs is unclear. Each breeder involved had different ideas about which breeds to use to get the desired characteristics – and few of those breeders kept exact records. In addition, nationalist based friction within the breed club led many to be vague when they made outcrosses to non-German breeds. We know that additional German hound blood was added to get the best possible nose, and it is likely that German retrieving breeds such as the pudel were added to enhance the natural retrieving instinct and love of water. French Braque and English Pointer blood was added to lengthen the leg and get the breed's head up. Rumor has it that even some Irish Setter was added by one noted breeder.

However, as with a Chinese puzzle, these crossbreeds at times had adverse affects on some of the characteristics the

Club desired, even as they added or strengthened other characteristics. English Pointer blood raised the nose, but it also adversely affected the breed's courage in dealing with predators, and diminished its desire to retrieve and its love of water. Additional time and inbreeding was necessary to wash out these undesirable characteristics while keeping the benefits of a high nose that the Pointer brought. Within the first fifteen years these breeders began producing dogs that started winning field trials against their British and French counterparts. In 1883, the famed German Shorthairs Nero and Treff won the German Derby against French and British dogs. While Hektor only a decade earlier was still stocky and hound like – in Nero and Treff we can clearly see the modern German Shorthair. By the time the new century rolled around, those German breeders had created the modern German Shorthaired pointer – a breed that was well on its way toward meeting that goal of the ultimate foot hunter's dog on which they had set their sights.

THE BREED SPREADS OUTSIDE GERMANY

The new breed began to attract attention in other European countries. Prior to World War I, German Shorthairs had spread to Austria, Denmark and the Scandinavian countries, and the Netherlands. After World War I, the breed continued to gain attention among hunters in Europe and beyond.

German immigrants brought their German Shorthairs with them as they moved to countries in South America. Where German immigrants settled in communities in Argentina and Chile, Paraguay, Uruguay and Brazil - hunters used their German Shorthairs to hunt the local game. German Shorthairs proved to be as adept at hunting the perdiz, zumbador, and other native game of South America as they had been hunting the partridge, quail, woodcock, and pheasant of Europe.

World War II brought cataclysmic destruction and ruin to much of Europe – and as human populations suffered so too did populations of hunting dogs. When food and medicine are in short supply, dogs have to survive, if they can, on what remains. The breeds of Germany and Central Europe (such as the Viszla and Czesky Fousek) suffered particularly drastic population declines. The German Shorthair suffered along with the rest. Not only did some noted breeders and lines disappear during the war – but even feeding dogs became difficult in some areas during the war and its aftermath. While the German Shorthair went into the War with healthy populations – it emerged with a population level that was a fraction of what it had been in the years prior to the war. Moreover, many allied troops stationed in Germany in the years after the war returned to their homes with German Shorthairs – sometimes from excellent bloodlines. As with other breeds, the loss of quality brood stock had a serious effect on a population whose gene pool had been so reduced.

The two decades after the end of World War II were decades of rebuilding for the breed in its native land. There had been such a loss of genetic diversity in German Shorthair populations in Germany that finding good brood stock that wasn't too closely related became difficult. One example of this problem involves the famous Axel von Wasserschling – perhaps the greatest stud of his time in Germany. Studs of his quality were so scarce in Germany that he was used by a large number of breeders. Unfortunately, this became so widespread that it became difficult to find blood that wasn't heavily influenced by Axel. This in turn made it increasingly difficult to avoid de facto inbreeding – and this began to cause genetic problems. Genetic maladies such as epilepsy, thyroid problems, and von Wildebrand's disease began to be seen in lines where they had been previously unknown. Breeders desperately began to search for "Axel frei" blood – and had to cast their eyes far and wide to find brood stock that would help them return to a healthy level of genetic diversity. Some argue that the German stock of German Shorthairs still suffer from the small gene pool and lack of genetic diversity that handicapped breeders in the post war period.

It is almost ironic that while the breed was struggling to regain its footing in the land of its birth – it was also establishing a foothold in new countries. The German Shorthair first showed up in Great Britain in the years of the Allied occupation of Germany – brought back by British

27

German Shorthairs are the most popular versatile breed in New Zealand. This is Fred, a NZ Shorthair owned by Margaret Cotton.

soldiers who served in the British Army on the Rhine. These soldiers were impressed by the hunting performance of German Shorthairs – and thought that the breed would be ideal for what the British call "rough shooting." Noted British hunters such as Michael Brander recognized the advantages of the breed – and began to talk up their attributes. While the British have long been far more comfortable exporting dog breeds rather than importing breeds from the Continent – the German Shorthair managed to establish itself with a dedicated group of hunters. From the UK, the German Shorthair then traveled down under to New Zealand, Australia, and South Africa – where it began impressing hunters. By the late 1960s or early 1970s it had became the most popular foot hunting pointing breed among hunters in Australia and New Zealand.

Today, the traditional German Shorthair is by registrations the most popular pointing dog among hunters throughout the world. While the breed is only the second most popular pointing breed in its country of origin (behind the German Wirehaired Pointer), it is the most popular pointing breed in much of the rest of Europe. In France, the home of the Brittany

28

and dozens of other famous pointing breeds – the German Shorthair is reportedly now the favorite breed of French hunters. The breed has won the hearts of hunters in Scandinavia, Central Europe, and even parts of Spain and Italy – the birthplaces of the original European pointing breeds. German Shorthairs are still the favorites of hunters in New Zealand, and those that remain in Australia – and have gained substantial popularity in South Africa. German Shorthairs are also one of the top hunting breeds in South America – from Argentina to Colombia. One can now see German Shorthairs hunting Andean Snipe and perdiz in the High Andes, quail in the Pampas of Argentina and Chile, and retrieving dove in the vast wheat fields of South America. Finally, German Shorthairs have become the most popular pointing breed among US hunters.

THE GERMAN SHORTHAIR IN THE UNITED STATES

The GSP first officially came to the US in 1925 when Dr. Thornton of Missoula, Montana imported a number of German Shorthairs from Austria. While there is scattered evidence that German immigrants may have brought their beloved German Shorthairs with them to America as early as the 1880s, Dr. Thornton is the first whose efforts are definitively documented. Having heard of the all around attributes of the breed, particularly the ability to handle a variety of birds such as pheasants and Hungarian partridges as well as waterfowl, Dr. Thornton decided to try some of the breed in his native Montana.

He soon became an avid advocate for the breed. In a 1926 issue of the American Field, Dr. Thornton wrote:

"The coat is longer than our English Pointer and very closely knit, resembling the coat of the hair seal.... They stand on strong legs and good feet, are short coupled, well muscled, deep barrel-shaped chest, characteristically expressive eyes and intelligent head; long, broad ears, regulation cropped tail; extremely elegant and smart in carriage and movement. On point they are strikingly beautiful. They begin retrieving as early as six weeks of age....

29

The German Shorthair became a favorite of US hunters in the "non-bobwhite" areas of the country because of its great nose, its quick intelligence, its ruggedness, and its adaptability.

They are naturally staunch (on point) and require little or no training. On game they can give one a real thrill. They will point any kind of game that will lie to cover and tree those that flush and take to the trees, where, as a rule, they bark 'treed'. I've used them in packs on coons just that way. After once they start pointing they will invariably back any other dog they see pointing, sometimes honoring from a distance of 150-200 yards, remaining absolutely steady until the bird is flushed. This backing instinct comes naturally and puppies need not be trained to honor.... As to speed and range they compare favorably with our English Pointers and Setters of the shooting-dog class. They seldom range farther than a quarter of a mile from the gunner. I have hunted them side by side with some of my fast Llewellins and they invariably located more birds.... They hunt heavy cover with ease and eagerness, naturally adapting their range to suit conditions. As retrievers they are at home on land or in water and they will locate dead or wounded game in the heaviest brush or briar...."

The breed proved so successful that other hunters around the U.S. began to take note. Hunters in Nebraska, Wisconsin, and Minnesota imported German Shorthairs – and the breed began to gain limited popularity among knowledgeable hunters. Dr. Thornton and early pioneers such as Ernst Rojem, Walter Mangold, and Joseph Burkhart created a Breed Club for the German Shorthair and in 1930 the breed was recognized by the AKC.

These states that proved such fertile ground for the German Shorthair in the US were areas where bobwhite had never been king, or where bobwhite had been replaced by "exotic" birds such as pheasants and chukars as the main choice of hunters. Indeed, German Shorthairs only started to make serious inroads into bobwhite country in the 1990s, and still remain relatively uncommon when compared to Pointers in many of the southern states.

In the early days it appeared that the German Shorthair would rapidly gain in popularity with hunters. However, the Depression limited the spread of "exotic" breeds such as the German Shorthair, and World War II made things German highly unpopular for many years after the war's end. It wasn't until the early 1960s that the German Shorthair began to gain truly widespread popularity as a hunting dog in the United States. The breed spread quickly from the upper Midwest to Washington and California, as well as Pennsylvania and the Atlantic states. From the west coast the breed spread out to the southwest and inter-mountain west. This spread was helped by great breeders producing outstanding hunting German Shorthairs – breeders such as Don Miner and Jake Huizenga in California, the Johns brothers in Pennsylvania, Ralph Park and Bob Holcomb in Washington, John Shattuck in Minnesota, the Shellenbargers of Gretchenhof kennels in California and many others.

In more modern times, the breed has been blessed with a few noted breeders that have continued to focus on producing outstanding hunting dogs – and some foundation dogs that somehow seem to wind up in the pedigree of many of the most outstanding hunters. Bob Check of Vom Enzstrand Kennels and Dr. Jim Reiser of Shooting Starr kennels are keeping up the long tradition of outstanding German Shorthairs coming out of Wisconsin. Just as Joe Furrow is doing so with his Hawkeye kennels in Iowa. Brenda Roe and Rick Hopkins with their Walnut Hill kennels are producing some great hunting GSPs out of Georgia. Cindy Stahle with her Honeyrun kennels is continuing the long Pennsylvania tradition of producing top quality Shorthairs. The Carters of Merrymeeting Kennels in Maine are also producing some fine traditional Shorthairs for hunters. All of these breeders, and many more, are standing on the shoulders of those great pioneers of the breed in the US that came before them – and producing German Shorthairs that are as good as any in the world.

As noted previously, the German Shorthair in the United States has become increasingly split since the 1980s between traditional hunting style German Shorthairs bred by breeders like those above, trial style German Shorthairs, German imports, and mixtures of the various strains. This means that identifying foundation dogs in the breed, great breeders, and outstanding lines has gotten far more complicated over the last twenty years.

Identifying such dogs is also extremely subjective, and something of a moving target as new blood comes in and old blood is diluted. Nevertheless, there are still a couple of dogs that stand out as relatively modern foundation dogs for hunting German Shorthairs in my opinion. It would not be unusual today to see these within the five-generation pedigree of a new pup. Of these, DC Hillhaven's Hustler is the one with which I have been most impressed – I love Hustler blood. A good amount of Hustler blood in the pedigree seems almost the hallmark of a good hunting GSP. DC Erik Von Enzstrand is another, older, dog that shows in the pedigree of some great traditional lines – as is DC Essers Duke Von Der Wildburg. Finally, there is a host of wonderful German KS dogs from the famed Hege Haus kennels – Malve, Elk, Fides and Zobel that often show up in some great hunting pedigrees.

Having said this, it is important to note a problem with focusing on such foundation dogs. Over the years, like many breeders, I have come to believe that it is actually the female

Greta von Geldie, a "Hustler" great granddaughter, shows some of the hunting prowess for which this blood is so famous.

that contributes more of the expressed genetic characteristics to the pups.

In golf they say you drive for show but you putt for dough. In breeding the sire's for show, the dam's for dough. Many German breeders also place great importance on the "mother line." There are detailed scientific reasons why this is likely to be true having to do with sex linked characteristics and complicated genetic theories – but rather than produce a scientific treatise, suffice it to say that I think that that this comes through strongly in the real world. Because studs can be mated to dozens of females in a fairly short time, it is the stud dogs that are invariably lauded as foundation dogs in the breed books. If, in fact, the females have more influence over the pups than the males – then you can see the weakness in this stud focused system. I've listed the dogs above because they appear to have some "prepotent" characteristics that seem to carry through regardless of the female – but it would be a mistake to limit your search exclusively to pedigrees containing the blood above.

One of the things that becomes immediately obvious as you consider how successful the German Shorthair has been in so many different countries and climates is the breed's tremendous adaptability. These different countries offer some of the most diverse hunting terrain, and encompass the widest variety of game birds and game animals on the planet –

Many experienced dog breeders believe that the dam contributes more to the expressed characteristics of a litter than the stud. The contributions of Annchen (rear) to her son Billy (front) and daughter Rosie (rear), are clear.

yet the German Shorthair has become popular with hunters in each one. This adaptability has literally been built into the breed in the physical, mental, and instinctive characteristics that those German creators instilled in the breed. The unsurpassed scenting abilities, the moderate range and pace, the intelligence and bidability, and the strong natural pointing and retrieving instincts remain constant wherever the breed is found. These characteristics enable the German Shorthair to effectively hunt a wide variety of game in a wide variety of terrains and climates.

The German Shorthair has earned its place in the hearts of hunters all over the world through its consistently outstanding performance in the hunting field, it's calm intelligence, it's courage, and it's loving, loyal disposition. It has done so without extensive breed promotion or publicity, and even, in the case of the United States, in the face of hostility from segments of the hunting dog establishment.

3

Physical Characteristics

The question of conformation was a key question for those German breeders who first created the German Shorthair. While form does follow function, it is equally true that function is affected by form. For example: a dog that is too small is not as effective in retrieving large game birds such as Geese and Swans, a dog that is too stocky does not cover ground as easily or quickly as one that is light and leggy, a dog that is too large can not work as effectively in close cover and requires more food and care, etc. The Germans therefore needed to come up with an ideal form for a dog they wanted to be an ideal hunting dog for a hunter on foot.

Thanks to the advice of Prince Albrecht zu Solms-Braunfeld, the form of the German Shorthair evolved organically. Prince Albrecht advised the group of breeders developing the new German Shorthair breed that they should focus on function in developing the breed, and let the form sort itself out. As a result, they wound up through trial and error with a form that is ideally suited for a versatile upland dog for a foot hunter.

The importance of conformation is widely misunderstood among hunters in the United States in particular. Many hunters believe that the breed standard is only important to those who participate in dog shows. Nothing could be farther from the truth. Form does indeed follow function. However, when you have developed a breed to the point it optimally performs the functions desired – form then becomes the safeguard that preserves the breed. When a breed reaches this point, it is not possible to make substantial changes to form without having a major impact on function.

Show breeders get blamed by hunters for "ruining" many hunting breeds. The Irish Setter, the Gordon Setter, the Weimeraner, and the American Cocker Spaniel are all examples of hunting breeds that in the United States were altered to the point that good hunting stock became extremely rare. Show breeders began to breed for exaggerated or irrelevant physical

Good conformation is essential to enable a hunting dog to function at its best. This is Wilhelm von Geldie (Billy) an excellent hunter bred and owned by the author.

characteristics that adversely impacted each breed's ability to hunt, and even mental stability in the case of American cocker spaniels and Irish Setters. Yet history shows that before these breeds began their decline – the breed standards were changed by the breed clubs in ways that adversely affected the breed's ability to perform its functions.

These changes were almost invariably made without significant opposition from hunters who considered conformation irrelevant. History has proved the price of such disregard for the breed standard and conformation. Hunters have had decades of work trying to bring these breeds back to their hunting roots with varying success – and many breeds look likely to have permanently split between show strains and hunting strains.

Fortunately, the German Shorthair has not gone down that route so far –and the breed standards remain true to the vision of the ultimate foot-hunting dog that inspired those early German breeders. The German Shorthair has three major breed standards – the German breed club standard that is also the international FCI standard; the American Kennel Club breed standard; and the Kennel Club of Great Britain standard. The latter two standards were directly derived from the original German standard.

In the case of the American standard, the AKC standard today differs only slightly from the German standard. The size listed in the American standard is smaller than the German standard, the tail is docked slightly shorter, and black is not listed as an acceptable color. When the American standard was first adopted in 1930 – black was a highly controversial topic in Germany. In order to darken the eyes of their stock, a number of breeders in Prussia had crossbred in Pointer blood from black colored Arkwright Pointers – introducing black into the GSP color spectrum. This was done over the objections of a good portion of the German breed club – so a separate stud book was created for these crossbred "Prussian Shorthairs" for a short time until the Pointer characteristics could be washed out and the stock be deemed "pure." Because black is a dominant color – the color survived this genetic washing. The Germans finally merged the two studbooks the year the American standard was adopted – so while black was eventually accepted as a legitimate GSP color by the Germans, the Americans had adopted the older color standard. There have been periodic attempts to change the American color standard for German Shorthairs to recognize black as an acceptable color (as does the rest of the world) but they have failed to date.

The GSP is fortunate in that no serious attempt has been made to substantially alter the breed standard in many years. Any hunter reading the breed standard would find little with which to disagree – the standard describes a healthy, sturdy hunting dog that would easily be able to perform the functions for which the German Shorthair was created. However, the standard does have at least one area in which it has never been clear and specific enough – and this unclear standard has had unfortunate results.

This weakness is the lack of a clear standard for the coat of the German Shorthair. The Germans who created the breed

Quincy, a black German Shorthair owned by Margaret Cotton. Black is an officially accepted German Shorthair color in every country but the United States.

gave it a specialized coat that has a number of advantages for a breed expected to work on both land and water. Unlike a typical Pointer coat – the German Shorthair coat has two layers. Close to the skin is an oily, wiry undercoat that makes the coat highly water resistant and insulates the dog in cold weather. The undercoat enables German Shorthairs to do cold-water retrieves in waterfowl season –and to work the uplands comfortably in temperatures that send other Shorthaired breeds home shivering.

My German Shorthairs will hunt without discomfort in temperatures that I find too cold to hunt comfortably - down to zero degrees Fahrenheit or below – thanks to the insulating properties of this undercoat. Germans used to compare this undercoat to seal's fur – both for its consistency and insulating properties in cold water. The density of this undercoat varies depending upon the climate in which the dog lives. In hotter weather the undercoat tends to get quite thin, while in colder weather it gets much thicker. However, a good Shorthair coat should always have some of this undercoat – even in mid summer in a hot climate.

You can easily tell if a Shorthair has this undercoat by brushing the dog. Strands of this fur-like undercoat should be easily visible on the brush. Shorthairs that lack this undercoat are said to have a "Pointer coat," which handicaps them in retrieving from cold water, handling cold weather, and working in rough terrain. Indeed, this undercoat is one of the key physical characteristics identifying a traditional German Shorthair from a Pointer crossbreed.

The second, outer, layer of a Shorthair's coat consists of tight, stiff guard hairs typically around ¾ of an inch in length. These guard hairs have a needle like shape that give them an irritating ability to work their way into carpets and upholstery. These tough guard hairs protect the dog from thorns and other environmental dangers.

In Arizona, there is a particularly nasty plant called catclaw that provides preferred cover for quail. Each twig and branch of this plant is covered by sharp curved thorns resembling cat's claws. Catclaw thickets can shred blue jeans and easily slice up bare skin. Most Pointers learn to avoid such thickets, and those that do work into them tend to get badly scratched. On the other hand, my German Shorthairs have always been able to work in even the thickest catclaw without getting badly scratched – a concrete example of the difference between a GSP coat and a Pointer coat. Together, these two layers give the Shorthair a versatile coat that enables it to work in a variety of terrains and climates I am convinced that this versatile coat is one of the key elements of the German Shorthair's popularity – enabling it to work equally well in both hot and cold weather.

I had a concrete demonstration of this remarkable ability a few years ago when I moved from Arizona to Wyoming. Although I lived in the mountains in Arizona where snow and cold temperatures were normal each winter – all of our hunting was done in relatively warm weather. We moved in the fall after we had a couple of days afield chasing desert quail in the warm October weather - and in a couple of months were face to face with the bitterness of a Wyoming winter.

In February, I agreed to go pheasant hunting with a friend. The temperature had been hovering just at freezing for two weeks – which didn't seem to be too nasty for hunting. However, the day before we went, the weather turned nasty with gusty winds, snow showers and temperatures in the teens. The area we hunted was the bottomlands on either side of Bear creek - a small creek about three feet deep and ten feet

A German Shorthair on point in a catclaw thicket. The German Shorthair coat provides protection from these nasty thorns

wide that meandered through the property. With the wind blowing, the wind chill factor pushed the temperature well below zero. The temperature was so cold that even with shooting gloves on, I cold not expose my hands to the wind for too long without fear of frostbite. Yet my German Shorthairs worked as though the temperature was in the fifties. They plunged in and out of the stream with complete unconcern – and found and pointed pheasants like normal, despite the miserable conditions.

Thus, I had seen my German Shorthairs hunting desert quail in temperatures in the seventies, and hunting pheasant in temperatures below zero, with equal skill and lack of discomfort within the space of four months. I can't think of many hunting dog breeds that would have performed as well in such extremes.

Aside from the weak standard for coat consistency, the three major standards describe a dog that is first and foremost a foot hunter's dog. The standards clearly refer the physical characteristics desired in the standard back to the hunting activities they are designed to facilitate. I think that few hunters would find anything with which to take exception in these breed standards. These three standards are listed below, with the German (FCI) standard first, the US standard second, and the UK standard third.

GERMAN SHORTHAIRED POINTER STANDARDS AROUND THE WORLD.

FCI (GERMAN) STANDARD:
GERMAN SHORTHAIRED POINTING DOG (DEUTSCH KURZHAAR)

TRANSLATION: Walter Schicker.

BRIEF HISTORICAL SUMMARY: The history of the German Shorthaired Pointing Dog starts with the dogs which were used for the hunt with nets on feathered game, especially in the Mediterranean countries, and in combination with falconry. Via France, Spain and Flanders the Pointers came to the German courts. The most important distinctive feature of these dogs was their pointing performance. After the first double-barreled gun was made (1750), a pointing dog was even more required. In full sight of the dog « game birds in flight » were shot. That was the beginning of the transition from a mere Pointer to a versatile gundog. As a fundamental basis for the structure and development of the breed the « Zuchtbuch Deutsch-Kurzhaar » (Studbook) has been published since 1897. It was Prince Albrecht zu Solms-Braunfeld who compiled breed characteristics, judging rules for conformation and finally also simple trial regulations for hunting dogs. Today the German Shorthaired Pointing Dog still passes through the filter of elaborated breeding- and trial regulations. The standard stipulates the constitution of the German Shorthaired Pointing Dog, as a versatile hunting dog, which enables him to perform all requirements in connection with hunting activities, even when advanced in age.

GENERAL APPEARANCE: A dog of noble and balanced appearance, the conformation of which ensures strength, endurance and speed. Proud attitude, smooth outlines, lean head, well carried tail, firm shiny coat and well reaching, harmonious strides emphasize its nobility.

41

IMPORTANT PROPORTIONS: Length of body should slightly exceed height at withers.

BEHAVIOUR / TEMPERAMENT: Firm, balanced, reliable, restrained temperament, neither nervous nor shy or aggressive.

HEAD: Lean, well defined, neither too light nor too heavy; as to strength and length it matches the substance and the sex of the dog.

CRANIAL REGION:

Skull: Moderately wide, flatly rounded, scarcely pronounced occipital bone, frontal furrow not too deep, and noticeably developed superciliary ridges.

Stop: Moderately defined.

FACIAL REGION:

Nose: Somewhat protruding. Nostrils sufficiently wide, broad and mobile. Basically brown, however black in black or black roan dogs. A flesh-coloured or spotted nose is only permissible in dogs with white as basic colour.

Muzzle: Long, broad, deep and strong in order to enable the dog's correct carrying of game. Viewed from the side the nasal bridge shows a slight curvature in all transitions from a nobly constructed ram's nose to a slight rise above the straight line - more prominent in males. A totally straight nasal bridge, although still acceptable, is less attractive; a concave bridge (dish-face) is a serious fault.

Lips: Tight fitting, not too pendulous, good pigmentation. The naso-labial line slopes almost vertically and then continues in a flat arch to the moderately pronounced corner of the lips.

Jaws/Teeth: Strong jaws with a perfect, regular and complete scissor bite. The upper incisors should reach over the lower incisors without gap and the teeth should be positioned vertically in the jaws. 42 sound teeth, in accordance with the teeth formula.

Cheeks: Strong, well muscled.

Eyes: Of medium size, neither protruding nor deep set. The ideal colour is dark brown. Eyelids tight fitting.

Ears: Moderately long, set on high and broad, flat and without twisting hanging down close to the head, bluntly rounded at the tip. Neither too fleshy nor too thin. When brought forward they are supposed to reach more or less the corner of the lips.

NECK: Length in harmony with general appearance of the dog, progressively thickening towards the body. Very muscular and slightly crested nape. Tight fitting skin of throat.

BODY:

Topline: Straight and slightly sloping.

Withers: Well defined.

Back: Firm and muscular. Vertebral processes should be covered by muscles.

Loin: Short, broad, muscular, straight or slightly arched. Transition from back to loin tight and well knit.

Croup: Broad and long enough, not abruptly slanting, but slightly slanting towards the tail, well muscled.

Chest: Somewhat deeper than broad with well defined forechest, with the sternum reaching back as far as possible. Sternum and elbow joint on the same level. Ribs well sprung, neither flat nor barrel-shaped. False ribs well reaching down.

Underline: With elegant arch, slightly tucked up towards rear, dry.

TAIL: Set high, strong at the root and then tapering, of medium length. About halfway docked for hunting purposes. At rest hanging down; in movement horizontal, neither carried too high above the backline nor extremely bent. (In countries where tail docking is prohibited by law, the tail can remain in its natural shape. It should reach down as far as the hocks and be carried straight or slightly sabre tail fashion).

LIMBS:

FOREQUARTERS:

General appearance: Viewed from the front, straight and parallel; viewed from the side, the legs are well placed under the body.

Shoulders: Shoulder blades well laid back, well attached to chest, and strongly muscled. Shoulder blade and upper arm well angulated.

Upper arm: As long as possible, well muscled and dry.

Elbow: Close but not too tight to body, neither turned in nor out, well set back.

Forearm: Straight and sufficiently muscled. Strong bone, not too coarse.

Pastern joint: Strong.

Pastern: Minimal angulation of pastern and forearm, never standing upright.

Forefeet: Round to spoon shaped, with well tight and adequately arched toes. Strong toenails. Tough, resistant pads. Feet set parallel, neither turned in nor out, in stance as well as in movement.

HINDQUARTERS:

General appearance: Viewed from behind straight and parallel. Good angulations in stifles and hocks, strong bone.

Upper thigh: Long, broad and muscular, with good angulation between pelvis and femur.

Stifle: Strong, with good angulation of upper- and lower thigh.

Lower thigh: Long, muscular with clearly visible tendons. Good angulation between lower thigh and hocks.

Hock joint: Strong.

Hocks: Strong, vertical.

Hind feet: Round to spoon shaped, with well tight and adequately arched toes. Strong toenails. Tough, resistant pads. Foot set parallel, neither turned in nor out, in stance as well as in movement.

GAIT: Well extended strides, with forceful propulsion from the hindquarters and adequate reach of the forelimbs. Front and hind legs moving straight and parallel. The dog is carrying himself in a proud attitude. Pacing gait is not desirable.

SKIN: Close and tight, not wrinkly.

COAT

Hair: Short and dense, rough and hard to the touch. Somewhat thinner and shorter on the head and ears, not remarkably longer at the underside of the tail. Should cover the whole body.

Colour: Solid brown, without markings. Brown with small white or flecked markings at chest and legs. Dark brown roan, with brown head, brown patches or specks. The basic colour of such a dog is not brown mixed with white or white with brown, but the coat shows such an even intensive mixture of brown and white which results in that kind of inconspicuous exterior of the dog ever so valuable for the practical hunt. At the inner sides of the hind legs as well as at the tip of the tail the colour is often lighter. Light brown roan with brown head, brown patches, specks or without patches. In this colouring the brown hairs are fewer, the white hairs are predominant. White with brown head markings, brown patches or specks. Black colour in the same nuances as the brown, respectively the brown roan colours. Yellow tan markings are permissible. Blaze, fleck and speckled flews are permissible.

SIZE:

Height at the withers: Dogs 62 to 66 cm. (24 to 26 inches)
Bitches 58 to 63 cm. (22 to 24 inches)

FAULTS: Any departure from the foregoing points should be considered a fault and the seriousness with which the fault should be regarded should be in exact proportion to its degree.

Faults in attitude, not according or typical to gender.

Muzzle too short.

Flews too heavy or too thin.

From the total of 4 PM 1 and 2 M3 only two teeth may be missing.

Eyes too light. Yellowish (bird of prey) eyes.

Ears too long, too short, too heavy, set on too narrow or twisted.

Loose skin at throat.

Slight roach back.

Rump too short.

Chest too deep.

Tail strongly bent or carried too high above the topline.

Elbows turned in or out. Feet turned in or out; forelegs standing close or wide.

Hindquarters too straight.

Slightly bow-legged, slightly cow-hocked or close hocks.

SERIOUS FAULTS:

Clumsy, lymphatic, coarse conformation.

Marked stop.

Flesh-coloured or flecked nose (except when basic colour of coat is white).

Snippy muzzle, concave bridge of the nose (dish-face).

Pincer bite or partial pincer bite (For dogs older than 4 years a so-called pincer bite due to age shall not affect evaluation as long as a « Deutsch-Kurzhaar-Club » has certified that at a previous show a correct bite was confirmed).

Distinct roach back, slight swayback.

Considerable lack in depth of chest. Poorly developed fore chest. Ribs too flat or barrel shaped.

Distinctly turned in or turned out elbows.

Weak and down on pasterns.

Pastern totally vertical.

Distinctly cow-hocked or bow-legged, in stance as well as in movement.

Overbuilt hindquarters.

Flat feet.

Spread toes.

Clumsy gait.

Deviation of more than 2 cm from the given height at the withers.

ELIMINATING FAULTS:

Aggressive or overly shy.

Distinctly non-typical gender characteristics.

Absence of more than 2 teeth from the total of 4 PM 1 and 2 M3. Absence of 1 tooth or more teeth other than PM 1 and M3. Non visible teeth have to be considered as missing except when certified by a « Deutsch-Kurzhaar-Club » that at a previous show or trial their existence was confirmed.

Overshot and undershot bite, wry mouth as well as all intergrades.

Any surplus teeth arranged outside the dental arch.

Cleft palate and hare lip.

Excessively loose eyelids, ectropion, entropion, distichiasis (double row of eyelashes).

Excessive swayback, malformation of the spine.

Any malformation of the chest, e.g. « clipped sternum » (short sternum blending abruptly into the abdominal line).

Dewclaws with or without bony skeleton.
Weak character.

Any dog clearly showing physical or behavioural abnormalities shall be disqualified.

N.B.: Male animals should have two apparently normal testicles fully descended into the scrotum.

AMERICAN KENNEL CLUB STANDARD - GERMAN SHORTHAIRED POINTER

GENERAL APPEARANCE

The German Shorthaired pointer is a versatile hunter, an all-purpose gun dog capable of high performance in field and water. The judgment of Shorthairs in the show ring reflects this basic characteristic. The overall picture which is created in the observer's eye is that of an aristocratic, well balanced, symmetrical animal with conformation indicating power, endurance and agility and a look of intelligence and animation. The dog is neither unduly small nor conspicuously large. It gives the impression of medium size, but is like the proper hunter, "with a short back, but standing over plenty of ground." Symmetry and field quality are most essential. A dog in hard and lean field condition is not to be penalized; however, overly fat or poorly muscled dogs are to be penalized. A dog well balanced in all points is preferable to one with outstanding good qualities and defects. Grace of outline, clean-cut head, sloping shoulders, deep chest, powerful back, strong quarters, good bone composition, adequate muscle, well carried tail and taut coat produce a look of nobility and indicate a heritage of purposefully conducted breeding. Further evidence of this heritage is movement which is balanced, alertly coordinated and without wasted motion.

Good conformation has benefits that last a lifetime. Even at 12 years of age Billy's fine conformation has enabled him to remain healthy and active in the field.

SIZE, PROPORTION, SUBSTANCE

Size--height of dogs, measured at the withers, 23 to 25 inches. Height of bitches, measured at the withers, 21 to 23 inches. Deviations of one inch above or below the described heights are to be severely penalized. Weight of dogs 55 to 70 pounds. Weight of bitches 45 to 60 pounds. Proportion--measuring from the fore chest to the rearmost projection of the rump and from the withers to the ground, the Shorthair is permissibly either square or slightly longer than he is tall. *Substance*--thin and fine bones are by no means desirable in a dog which must possess strength and be able to work over any type of terrain. The main importance is not laid so much on the size of bone, but rather on the bone being in proper proportion to the body. Bone structure too heavy or too light is a fault. Tall and leggy dogs, dogs which are ponderous because of excess substance, doggy bitches, and bitchy dogs are to be faulted.

HEAD

The head is clean-cut, is neither too light nor too heavy, and is in proper proportion to the body. The eyes are of medium size, full of intelligence and expression, good-humored and yet radiating energy, neither protruding nor sunken. The eye is almond shaped, not circular. The preferred color is dark brown. Light yellow eyes are not desirable and are a fault. Closely set eyes are to be faulted. China or wall eyes are to be disqualified. The ears are broad and set fairly high, lie flat and never hang away from the head. Their placement is just above eye level. The ears when laid in front without being pulled, should extend to the corner of the mouth. In the case of heavier dogs, the ears are correspondingly longer. Ears too long or fleshy are to be faulted. The skull is reasonably broad, arched on the side and slightly round on top. Unlike the Pointer, the median line between the eyes at the forehead is not too deep and the occipital bone is not very conspicuous. The foreface rises gradually from nose to forehead. The rise is more strongly pronounced in the dog than in the bitch. The jaw is powerful and the muscles well developed. The line to the forehead rises gradually and never has a definite stop as that of the Pointer, but rather a stop-effect when viewed from the side, due to the position of the eyebrows. The muzzle is sufficiently long to enable the dog to seize game properly and be able to carry it for a long time. A pointed muzzle is not desirable. The depth is in the right proportion to the length, both in the muzzle and in the skull proper. The length of the muzzle should equal the length of skull. A dish-shaped muzzle is a fault. A definite Pointer stop is a serious fault. Too many wrinkles in the forehead is a fault. The nose is brown, the larger the better, and with nostrils well opened and broad. A spotted nose is not desirable. A flesh colored nose disqualifies. The chops fall away from the somewhat projecting nose. Lips are full and deep yet are never flewy. The teeth are strong and healthy. The molars intermesh properly. The bite is a true scissors bite. A perfect level bite is not desirable and must be penalized. Extreme overshot or undershot disqualifies.

NECK, TOPLINE, BODY

The neck is of proper length to permit the jaws reaching game to be retrieved, sloping downwards on beautifully curving lines. The nape is rather muscular, becoming gradually larger toward the shoulders. Moderate throatiness is permitted. The skin is close and tight. The chest in general gives the impression of depth rather than breadth; for all that, it is in correct proportion to the other parts of the body. The chest reaches down to the elbows, the ribs forming the thorax show a rib spring and are not flat or slab-sided; they are not perfectly round or barrel-shaped. The back ribs reach well down. The circumference of the thorax immediately behind the elbows is smaller than that of the thorax about a hand's breadth behind elbows, so that the upper arm has room for movement. Tuck-up is apparent. The back is short, strong, and straight with a slight rise from the root of the tail to the withers. The loin is strong, is of moderate length, and is slightly arched. An excessively long, roached or swayed back must be penalized. The hips are broad with hip sockets wide apart and fall slightly toward the tail in a graceful curve. A steep croup is a fault. The tail is set high and firm, and must be docked, leaving approximately 40% of its length. The tail hangs down when the dog is quiet and is held horizontally when he is walking. The tail must never be curved over the back toward the head when the dog is moving. A tail curved or bent toward the head is to be severely penalized.

FOREQUARTERS

The shoulders are sloping, movable, and well covered with muscle. The shoulder blades lie flat and are well laid back nearing a 45 degree angle. The upper arm (the bones between the shoulder and elbow joint) is as long as possible, standing away somewhat from the trunk so that the straight and closely muscled legs, when viewed from the front, appear to be parallel. Elbows which stand away from the body or are too close result in toes turning inwards or outwards and must be faulted. Pasterns are strong, short and nearly vertical with a slight spring. Loose, short-bladed or straight shoulders must be faulted. Knuckling over is to be faulted. Dewclaws on the forelegs may be removed. The feet are compact, close-knit and round to spoon-shaped. The toes are sufficiently arched and heavily nailed. The pads are strong, hard and thick.

HINDQUARTERS

Thighs are strong and well muscled. Stifles are well bent. Hock joints are well angulated and strong with straight bone structure from hock to pad. Angulation of both stifle and hock joint is such as to achieve the optimal balance of drive and traction. Hocks turn neither in nor out. Cowhocked legs are a serious fault.

COAT

The hair is short and thick and feels tough to the hand; it is somewhat longer on the underside of the tail and the back edges of the haunches. The hair is softer, thinner and shorter on the ears and the head. Any dog with long hair in the body coat is to be severely penalized.

COLOR

The coat may be of solid liver or a combination of liver and white such as liver and white ticked, liver patched and white ticked, or liver roan. A dog with any area of black, red, orange, lemon or tan, or a dog solid white will be disqualified.

GAIT

A smooth lithe gait is essential. It is to be noted that as gait increases from the walk to a faster speed, the legs converge beneath the body. The tendency to single track is desirable. The forelegs reach well ahead as if to pull in the ground without giving the appearance of a hackney gait. The hindquarters drive the back legs smoothly and with great power.

TEMPERAMENT

The Shorthair is friendly, intelligent, and willing to please. The first impression is that of a keen enthusiasm for work without indication of nervous or flighty character.

DISQUALIFICATIONS

China or wall eyes.

Flesh colored nose.

Extreme overshot or undershot.

A dog with any area of black, red, orange, lemon, or tan, or a dog solid white.

Approved August 11, 1992.

Effective September 30, 1992

KENNEL CLUB OF GREAT BRITAIN BREED STANDARD – GERMAN SHORTHAIRED POINTER

GENERAL APPEARANCE

Noble, steady dog showing power, endurance and speed, giving the immediate impression of an alert and energetic dog whose movements are well co-ordinated. Of medium size, with a short back standing over plenty of ground. Grace of outline, clean-cut head, long sloping shoulders, deep chest, short back, powerful hindquarters, good bone composition, adequate muscle, well carried tail and taut coat.

CHARACTERISTICS

Dual purpose Pointer/Retriever, very keen nose, perseverance in searching and initiative in game finding, excellence in field, a naturally keen worker, equally good on land and water.

TEMPERAMENT

Gentle, affectionate and even-tempered. Alert, biddable and very loyal.

HEAD AND SKULL

Clean-cut, neither too light nor too heavy, well proportioned to body. Skull sufficiently broad and slightly round. Nasal bone rising gradually from nose to forehead (this more pronounced in dogs) and never possessing a definite stop, but when viewed from side a well defined stop effect due to position of eyebrows. Lips falling away almost vertically from somewhat protruding nose and continuing in a slight curve to corner of mouth. Lips well developed, not over hung. Jaws powerful and sufficiently long to enable the dog to pick up and carry game. Dish-faced and snipy muzzle undesirable. Nose solid brown or black depending on coat colour. Wide nostrils, well opened and soft.

EYES

Medium size, soft and intelligent, neither protruding nor too deep-set. Varying in shades of brown to tone with coat. Light eye undesirable. Eyelids should close properly.

EARS

Broad and set high; neither too fleshy nor too thin, with a short, soft coat; hung close to head, no pronounced fold, rounded at tip and reaching almost to corner of mouth when brought forward.

MOUTH

Teeth sound and strong. Jaws strong, with a perfect, regular and complete scissor bite, i.e. upper teeth closely overlapping lower teeth and set square to the jaws.

NECK

Moderately long, muscular and slightly arched, thickening towards shoulders. Skin not fitting too loosely.

FOREQUARTERS

Shoulders sloping and very muscular, top of shoulder blades close; upper arm bones, between shoulder and elbow, long. Elbows well laid back, neither pointing outwards nor inwards. Forelegs straight and lean, sufficiently muscular and strong, but not coarse-boned. Pasterns slightly sloping.

BODY

Chest must appear deep rather than wide but in proportion to rest of body; ribs deep and well sprung, never barrel-shaped nor flat; back ribs reaching well down to tuck-up of loins. Chest measurement immediately behind elbows smaller than about a hand's breadth behind elbows, so that upper arm has freedom of movement. Firm, short back, not arched. Loin wide and slightly arched; croup wide and sufficiently long, neither too heavy nor too sloping starting on a level with back and sloping gradually towards tail. Bones solid and strong. Skin should not fit loosely or fold.

HINDQUARTERS

Hips broad and wide, falling slightly towards tail. Thighs strong and well muscled. Stifles well bent. Hocks square with body and slightly bent, turning neither in nor out. Pasterns nearly upright.

FEET

Compact, close-knit, round to spoon-shaped, well padded, turning neither in nor out. Toes well arched with strong nails.

TAIL

Previously customarily docked.
Docked: Starts high and thick growing gradually thinner, customarily docked to medium length by two fifths to half its length. When quiet, tail carried down; when moving, horizontally. Never held high over back or bent.
Undocked: Moderately long, not reaching below hocks. Strong at root, becoming gradually thinner. Carried horizontally or just below line of back.

GAIT/MOVEMENT

Smooth, lithe gait essential. As gait increases from walk to a faster speed, legs converge beneath body (single tracking). Forelegs reach well ahead, effortlessly covering plenty of ground with each stride and followed by hind legs, which give forceful propulsion.

COAT

Short, flat and coarse to touch, slightly longer under tail.

COLOUR

Solid liver, liver and white spotted, liver and white spotted and ticked, liver and white ticked, solid black or black and white same variations (not tri-colour).

SIZE

Dogs: minimum height 58 cms (23 ins) at withers, maximum height 64 cms (25 ins) at withers. Bitches: minimum height 53 cms (21 ins) at withers, maximum height 59 cms (23 ins) at withers.

FAULTS

Any departure from the foregoing points should be considered a fault and the seriousness with which the fault should be regarded should be in exact proportion to its degree and its effect upon the health and welfare of the dog

NOTE

Male animals should have two apparently normal testicles fully descended into the scrotum.

Last Updated - September 2007

While good conformation is not a guarantee of the other instincts needed to make a fine hunting dog – it is still vital. As long as a German Shorthair fits the breed standard, it will have the physical tools to do its job. Parents that have good conformation as outlined above are likely to throw pups that do as well. Therefore, as you search for a pup that will have good conformation within the breed standard, you should use the breed standard when examining the parents as well.

4

Finding Your Pup

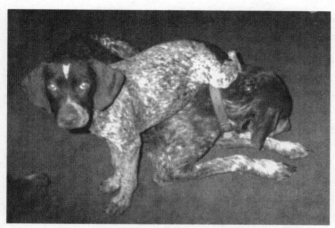

It takes more willpower than most of us have to resist a cutie like this. That's why its important to do your homework before you see a puppy.

The first thing you need to know about buying a puppy is that puppies are a trap. There is no such thing as an ugly German Shorthair puppy. They are adorable, loving and playful. Unless you have an iron will, if you see a puppy, if you smell that wonderful puppy breath, you will go home with a puppy. It won't matter whether the pup comes from stock that hasn't pointed a bird since Kennedy was president, whether the stock has the temperament of Cujo, whether the first time you release the pup in the field is likely to be the last time you see it. All you will see is those two soulful puppy eyes, that puppy button nose, and that little pink tongue and you will be hooked. The problem with all of this is that you will be stuck with the consequences of whatever decision you make for the next twelve to fifteen years – so an impulse buy is one that you may regret for a long time. This is why you need to wait until the very last step to see the puppy. The rule of thumb for finding a puppy is: first pick the type of Shorthair you are looking for, then pick the breeder, then the litter, then finally go and pick the puppy.

Over the years I have come to believe that about 90% of what goes into making a great hunting dog is genetic. Great hunting German Shorthairs come from great hunting stock.

Modern science tends to back up that assertion. The more we learn about genetics and the influence of genes on our physical and mental makeup – the more it shows that genes have an enormous influence over almost every aspect of our existence. We now know that individual genes and combinations of genes not only control physical characteristics, they regulate brain chemistry and function, and a whole range of instinctual behaviors. So not only is the physical conformation of a pup determined by its genetic inheritance, it also gets its pointing and retrieving instinct, temperament, intelligence, and a host of other personality characteristics from its parents. Essentially, a puppy is the sum total of the genetic inheritance it has received from its parents and their ancestors. You want to make sure that genetic inheritance is the best available – and to do that requires some thought and research.

When it comes to German Shorthairs we want to make sure that any pup has the full inheritance of genetic traits that have led to the breed being identified as "the ideal dog for the foot hunter." It's useful, before we begin our search, to get a clear idea of what those characteristics are.

Conformation:

The Germans who developed the German Shorthair devoted a lot of time and effort to developing a breed with the conformation to best do the jobs required of a versatile foot hunting dog. They developed a dog with significant differences from the English Pointers and Setters of the time. They gave the German Shorthair a length of leg and short coupling that allows it to work in uplands all day at a moderate range and pace. Anyone who has closely watched a Shorthair work will note the impressive amount of ground covered with a minimum of effort. Those breeders also gave it a deep chest rather than a classic barrel chest to enable it to have the wind to work all day while also giving the dog's front legs freedom of movement for swimming. The deep chest also allows the Shorthair to ride a little higher in the water to better see downed waterfowl. They gave it the size to retrieve geese and dispatch foxes and vermin – but kept it small enough to be nimble in the uplands. They gave it a strong, muscular neck to facilitate retrieving and carrying heavy game and the webbed feet of a retriever to facilitate swimming and water work. They gave the German Shorthair a coat that requires little maintenance, is short enough to let it work comfortably in warm climes but thick enough to let it retrieve comfortably from cold water and turn aside thorns. Finally, they gave it the proportions and symmetry that make the breed so beautiful.

The breed standard has remained relatively unchanged since the modern German Shorthair was developed, and continues to be the best guide to proper conformation – so we would like to see our dog have good conformation within the breed standard.

Nose:

We want a dog with an excellent nose. If I had to identify the single most important characteristic of a great hunting dog – it would be nose. The dog that consistently finds game where other dogs can't is the one I want to be hunting with. However, the question of nose is a bit complex. It used to be thought that nose was a physical characteristic – that some dog's noses were simply more sensitive than others. We now know that isn't true. Studies done by military scientists in various countries attempting to analyze the capacity of dogs to sniff out explosives have found that, with the exception of the pug nosed breeds, there isn't any significant difference in the ability of various breed's noses to gather scent. In fact, the ability of the sensors in a dog's nose to gather scent is little short of amazing. Dogs can literally differentiate individual molecules with their noses. What differs between breeds and individuals is how that scent is processed in the brain and what reactions are triggered.

The threshold at which some dogs key on tiny whiffs of scent, follow them to their source, and then hold the birds that released the scent under point varies from dog to dog and individual to individual. We call this nose, and while it isn't a physical characteristic as we used to believe – it still is a genetic trait that is passed down through inheritance. German Shorthairs have a reputation for outstanding noses because of the genetic inheritance given them by those old Germans who placed great importance on the quality of their breed's nose. We want to ensure that our pup comes from parents that exhibit the kind of "nose" for which the breed has long been famous.

Natural Pointing and Retrieving Instincts:

Even small Shorthair puppies will often show strong natural pointing instincts

We want a dog with strong natural pointing and retrieving instincts. German Shorthair pups will typically start retrieving objects at an early age – as early as five to six weeks in many cases. Because retrieving is a cooperative activity, strong natural retrieving instincts are also a good indication of a cooperative nature. While pointing doesn't typically manifest itself without an external stimulus – this instinct also tends to show up at an early age in German Shorthairs. Pups will often point grasshoppers, sparrows, butterflies, and other objects from the time they are six or seven weeks of age.

Ability to Learn and Cooperate:

We want a dog that is cooperative and biddable. These phrases are often used in an extremely cavalier manner. I once had an avid and experienced field trialer turn to me and say "isn't it amazing how cooperative and biddable this dog is?" about a dog that was running full speed a mile away and accelerating like a rocket while ignoring its handler completely. That didn't fit my definition of either cooperative or biddable, but it did his.

Cooperative, when we are discussing dogs refers to the package of social traits that enable a dog to work and hunt successfully within the pack structure. If we think of wolves, the dog's closest relative, then we see a majority of wolves live within a pack structure as individual parts of a communal society. The cooperativeness that enables them to live and hunt as part of a social group is the cooperativeness that we are discussing when we talk about dogs. These are primal canine instincts that are very much rooted in the dog's natural existence. A cooperative dog is a dog that is willing to work/hunt in cooperation with others within the pack; that pays attention to the others in the pack, communicates and coordinates its movements and actions with them; that focuses on the pack leader and willingly takes direction; and that develops social bonds within the group. These are the traits that enable a wolf pack to hunt and bring down game much larger than they are – and to survive in harsh environments. This also enables a hunting dog to hunt as part of a team with the hunter, keying movement to the movement of the hunter, and taking non-verbal cues and directions as well as verbal commands.

Not all wolves have these characteristics. Everyone has heard of "lone wolves" who either leave or are banished from the pack and spend their days in an independent, solitary existence. Sometimes these wolves join other packs, sometimes they find mates and start their own packs, and often they simply live as solitary rovers. These extremes of natural canine behavior – cooperativeness and solitary independence are mirrored in characteristics we see in our hunting dogs.

We will discuss this issue at greater length in other parts of this book, but for now suffice it to say that cooperativeness is a basic instinct, but not a universal instinct, among our hunting dogs. You have to actively seek cooperativeness in the genetic makeup of your pup – and you want to see it manifested in both parents. Thanks to those field trialers and other advocates of extreme independence in pointing dogs who have had a strong impact on the German Shorthair over the past decade or so, you can no longer merely assume that cooperativeness will be part of the package.

When many trainers speak of a biddable dog, they are incorrectly referring to dog that is obedient, that does what it is told. In fact, bidability refers to the desire to please and eagerness to learn as well as the willingness to comply. A biddable dog is one that willingly and even eagerly obeys, and eagerly learns new tasks. While hard to explain, the difference between a biddable dog and one that is simply obedient is easy to see in practice.

Temperament:

We also want a dog that has a good temperament. For the purposes of picking a pup let's say that we want a dog that will make a good family companion, that is friendly and intelligent, loyal and cooperative. We also want a dog that has a calm disposition – capable of sitting still in a duck blind or laying quietly at their owner's feet in the evening. We don't want a dog that is hyperactive, has too short of an attention span, is either too bold or too timid, too active or lethargic, or aggressive to humans or other dogs.

Range and Pace:

We want our German Shorthair to have a moderate range and pace. There are a number of reasons for this. The first is that range is directly related to cooperativeness. If we can imagine a spectrum with extremes of independence and cooperativeness at each end– the pointing breeds fall in the space between the two extremes. We want our hunting dogs to have a degree of independence – to have a bit of that lone wolf-in order to get them to range out and search for game.

At the same time, we want a dog that will not just take off – but one that will check back regularly for direction and coordinate its movements to those of the hunter. The big running All Age Pointers and Setters are all highly independent dogs. By the same token, the retrieving breeds tend to be extremely cooperative. Traditional German Shorthairs tend to have personalities that fall somewhere in between these two.

The relatively high level of cooperativeness of German Shorthairs when compared to the All Age Pointers and Setters is what accounts for the German Shorthairs reputation for being easy to train and handle, and for its bidability. By the same token, the independence gives the German Shorthair its inquisitiveness and urge to search and range away from the gunner.

The end result of this combination between cooperativeness and independence in the German Shorthair is a dog that typically ranges between 50 yards and 300 yards depending upon the terrain and cover. In open cover and flat country, where the dog can maintain eye and ear contact with the hunter at a great range – the German Shorthair will feel comfortable working at ranges up to 300 yards or more. In more broken, brushy country, the German Shorthair will have to work closer to the hunter to maintain the desired degree of contact. In grouse forests and similar terrain German Shorthairs may work as close as 50 yards to the hunter in order to be able to maintain contact.

This moderate range and pace has other practical benefits for the hunter. As noted above, a dog's ability to pick up faint scent is affected by physical factors such as respiratory rates, temperature, and the moistness of the nasal cavity. For the hunter, this means that a dog that is running fast is at a significant handicap when it comes to fine scenting. A dog working at a moderate pace is working at a better speed to pick up faint scent. That moderate pace also enables the dog to conserve energy and work for longer periods without injury or debilitation. Finally, the moderate range enables the German Shorthair to coordinate closely and work as a team with the hunter – the quality known as hunting for the gun.

FINDING THE RIGHT LITTER

The real heart of the matter when it comes to finding the perfect pup is finding the right breeder and the right litter. Compared to those two tasks, actually picking the pup is the fun and easy part. Each year roughly 14,000 German Shorthairs are registered with the American Kennel Club, with perhaps another 2,500 registered with other registries such as the Field Dog Stud Book and the North American Versatile Hunting Dog Association. Assuming an average litter size of eight pups, this means that approximately 2000 German Shorthaired Pointer litters are whelped in the US each year.

The key to finding a great hunting dog is finding a great litter. All of these pups turned out to be outstanding hunters

A liberal estimate would be, therefore, that someone searching for a German Shorthaired Pointer puppy would have a choice of dealing with more than 1,000 breeders producing German Shorthairs across a spectrum of types that differ as much between their extremes as German Shorthairs do from other breeds. At a guess from what I've seen in recent years, I would say that perhaps one third of those breeders are focused on producing traditional style hunting German Shorthairs with the characteristics above, another thirty five percent are focused on producing German Shorthairs for competition that often lack many of the characteristics above; and the remainder are casual breeders or breeders focused primarily on the pet trade or who lack any specific focus at all.

Sorting through this abundance of breeders producing German Shorthairs with different characteristics requires some research and some investigation. The first thing to recognize is that genetics is a science based upon odds and probabilities. The fact that a puppy comes from parents that are outstanding hunters, who in turn come from generations of fine hunting Shorthairs, is not an absolute guarantee that the pup will be a fine hunter – but it's as close to an absolute guarantee as you will get. By the same token, if you are looking to get a puppy suitable for All Age trials (where dogs are expected to have a high degree of independence and work at ranges of a half mile or more) from such a litter – you are making a sucker bet. The odds are you aren't going to get the type of pup you want. The point is that while there are exceptions – you tend to get the type of dog that you are breeding for. If you want to find a good hunting pup your best odds are looking for breeders that are trying to produce outstanding hunting dogs – not competition dogs or pets.

The breeding business is a competitive business – and as with any business in which people make a living there tends to be a lot of misinformation and exaggerated claims bandied about. Big kennel breeders will often say that you shouldn't buy from smaller breeders because they don't know what they are doing. Smaller breeders say that you shouldn't buy from the Big kennels because they are little more than puppy mills – focused on cranking out a quantity of pups rather than maximizing their quality. All of this can make it quite confusing for someone looking to buy their first German Shorthair.

The first piece of advice I have is to ignore such backbiting completely. Some of the best German Shorthairs in US history have come from committed hobby breeders and hunters who only bred a litter every few years to get their next generation of hunting dogs. Don't be afraid of talking to breeders who advertise in the local paper, or on the bulletin board at the local hunting store. Some of the best hunting stock comes from such breeders. Similarly, many larger kennels have built a solid reputation based on producing quality pups. The important point is that whatever breeders you locate should be focused on breeding traditional hunting German Shorthairs first and foremost and on bettering the breed.

Where do you find such breeders? Well, the best place to find a breeder is through a reference from an experienced hunter who does the type of hunting you want to do and who has a dog from the breeder he recommends. The best scenario would be if you also have a chance to hunt over this dog and to get to know it so that you are sure that you would want a similar pup. Without the first hand knowledge acquired from being around a dog, and hunting with a dog in the field, then you are going to have to rely on what lawyers call "hearsay" evidence about the quality of breeders. Knowledgeable hunters and hunting guides might recommend certain breeders; participants on hunting dog bulletin boards on the internet might provide different recommendations, etc. You also might find leads in advertisements in the local newspaper, on the bulletin board at local hunting shops, etc. You are NOT likely to find a good German Shorthair in a pet shop – and I would never recommend purchasing a pup from such a business. In 35 years with the breed I can think of no reputable breeder producing quality hunting dogs that I know who would sell their pups in such a venue.

Once you have some leads on potential breeders – whether they own major professional kennels, or whether it's simply a hunter producing a litter in his back yard, your research begins. The first thing you want to do is to contact the breeder and ask them about the type of German Shorthairs they are producing and any potential upcoming litters. All good breeders have a breeding philosophy – a clear picture of the type of dogs they are seeking to produce and how they intend to produce them. The secret is to get a breeder to talk about their breeding philosophy instead of simply telling you what you want to hear.

To do this, it's important to let the breeder talk with a minimum of prompting from you. Ask the breeder to talk about their breeding philosophy and the type of German Shorthairs they are producing. Don't tell them the type of German Shorthair you are seeking because it is likely to color their responses to you – if only subconsciously.

Start with open ended questions that allow them to fully describe to you the German Shorthairs they are trying to produce. As the discussion proceeds – ask more specific questions. Ask them if they hunt their Shorthairs, and if so whether they do the type of hunting you do. Have them tell you about their experiences hunting with their Shorthairs. Do they hunt waterfowl as well as upland birds, and do they hunt with their Shorthairs cooperatively or do they simply follow their

66

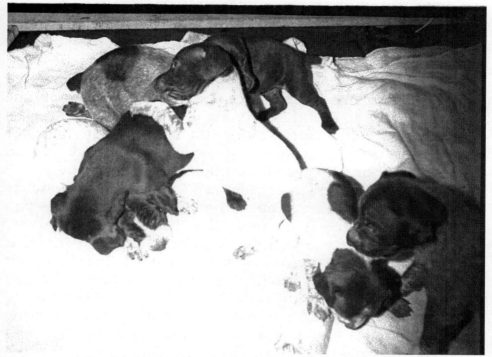

A competent breeder should have a very good idea of the type of dogs that their pups will grow up to be based upon the genetics of the dam and stud.

dogs around? Try and pin down issues such as range and pace, temperament around other dogs as well as children, natural pointing and retrieving instinct, whether the Shorthairs will back naturally, and the quality of the dog's nose?

Any good breeder should have a very good idea of these attributes if only because pups are a mixture of the genes of their parents, and the breeder should know these qualities in the parents. If you find a breeder that can't, or won't answer these questions even generally – then steer clear. This is a breeder that doesn't know their business or is seeking to hide something.

Only after you've had the breeder tell you that they are seeking to breed the type of German Shorthair that you are seeking should you tell the breeder about the characteristics you are seeking in your pup. You can then discuss more specifics about what you are looking for and whether the breeder feels that their Shorthairs will fit the bill.

Don't expect this to be a one sided interview. A good breeder will also ask you questions to ensure that their pups are going to a good home. Be prepared to discuss in some detail the living arrangements you have for the pup, the amount of time you will be able to spend in training and working the pup, the nature of your family, and whether the dog will be an inside or outside dog, etc. Just as you are seeking a good pup, a good breeder is seeking to place their pups with a good family.

Once you've found a breeder who's philosophy matches yours, and who appears to be producing your dream pup – you need to do some research. Genetics is governed by probabilities. If you are buying a pup from a stud and dam that have had litters together previously – then it is probable that pups from the new litter will have the same characteristics (and problems) as pups from previous litters. So you should ask the breeder for references from hunters who own pups from the previous litters –and you need to call and talk to these references.

You need to ask for specifics in terms of range, nose, pointing and retrieving instincts, bidability, cooperativeness, temperament, and health. Remember that some genetic maladies don't show up until a dog is a year old or older. Things like epilepsy, hip dysplasia, thyroid problems, diabetes, etc. often won't be evident in dogs as puppies – even if they will show the maladies later. So it's useful, if possible, to get references from hunters who may have pups from previous litters that may now be two years of age or older.

If the hunters you speak with tell you that in fact the breeder is turning out the kind of pups they say, that they are good hunting dogs and family companions, and that they are in good health and free of genetic maladies –then you are ready to take the next step.

Unless you are very familiar with a great number of German Shorthair foundation lines and dogs – a pedigree will be of limited use in selecting a pup. While the pedigree is an outline of the pup's genetic inheritance - without knowing the dogs involved and their characteristics- it provides only a modest amount of useful information.

Perhaps the most useful bit of information a pedigree provides is that it will quickly tell how inbred, and therefore how likely to have genetic problems, a dog is. Genetic maladies are typically (though not always) carried on recessive genes that become more likely to express themselves in dogs that have a low degree of genetic diversity. This is a fancy way of saying that if a dog has a pedigree where you see breedings that mated father to daughter; mother to son; or brother to sister; or where a single dog appears more than twice in the second generation or more than four times in the third generation – you are at a significantly higher risk for genetic maladies and abnormalities. Breeding that tends to mate closely related dogs – sometimes called linebreeding – is favored by some breeders because it increases the chances that their pups will have characteristics very similar to those of their parents. However, as noted above, it also increases the probability of genetic problems – so I would avoid pedigrees with a large number of matings of directly related dogs.

Another useful bit of information to be gleaned from a pedigree is a general overview of the dog's ancestry. As mentioned before, without a thorough knowledge of the individual dogs contained in the pedigree it isn't really possible to get a full picture of the dog's genetic makeup. However, it is possible to get hints. For example, if you see a pedigree where you see a large number of FC titles before dogs' names (field trial champions) without a lot of other titles then it is likely you are looking at a field trial strain of German Shorthairs with all that might entail. Similarly, if you see a large number of CH titles (show champions) before the names of dogs in the pedigree, without a lot of other titles, then it is likely you are looking at a show strain of German Shorthairs with what that might entail. At this point I should note that over the years I have found some good traditional hunting German Shorthairs from show stock – though again you can also find some dogs with limited hunting instincts as well.

Most GSP pedigrees nowadays will have some field trial and show champions somewhere in the pedigree. When I look at a pedigree I prefer to see a balance between the two because I believe that the show blood with its emphasis on traditional conformation tends to offset the trial blood with its emphasis on run. Having said this, there are also some titles that I tend to look for in a pedigree.

The first is KS or Kurzhaar Sieger – the German champion title. The Germans don't believe in field trialing in the American style. Instead, they have a rigorous testing system in which all Shorthairs have to be evaluated before they can be bred. This testing combines elements that test field performance on land and water, tracking, obedience, temperament, and conformation among other things. Every Shorthair is awarded a score for a variety of characteristics. Dogs that fail to achieve a passing score are forbidden to be bred. Dogs that achieve top marks are awarded the KS title. It is fairly common to find such German imports in the pedigree of traditional German Shorthairs. Another European title that might show up is the WS or Welt Sieger title. This is a primarily show title that is awarded to European Shorthairs with outstanding conformation.

The second title is the American DC or Dual Champion title. This was once the apex of the German Shorthair world and a sign that there was no great split between the field and show strains within the German Shorthair breed. Some of the truly great examples in the history of the German Shorthair Breed have been Dual Champions – though today there is a significant split in the breed and the DC title is no longer the ultimate guarantee of traditional qualities that it used to be. Still, the strong field trial strains – the ones that have the most Pointer-like characteristics – tend to lack the conformation to win show titles. This means that DCs are still likely to have more traditional GSP characteristics than simple FCs.

If the pedigree doesn't ring any alarm bells, and the references check out – it's time to make arrangements to visit the breeder. When you talk with the breeder let them know that you not only want to look at the puppies, but also the dam and stud if possible. Ask if it might be possible to see the dam and stud in the field (on birds if possible) – or at the very least to interact with them. The reason for this is that the pup is a mix of the traits of the dam and stud – if you see undesirable traits in the dam and stud there is a good chance you will see them in your pup. Remember, that if the dam is still nursing it is likely that you will not see her at her best. As with new human mothers she may be harassed and tired, and you should take this into account as you assess her. Be that as it may, the more you can see of the dam and stud, the more you can verify that they have the characteristics and temperament you want in a dog – the more likely you are going to get them in your pup.

Once you feel comfortable about the breeder, the litter, the pedigree, the dam and stud then you finally get to the fun part – picking a pup. There are dozens of ways of picking an individual puppy – and if you have done your homework and chosen a good litter, each pup is likely to have the characteristics you want. That means that any method with which you feel comfortable is likely to produce a good pup.

I have always preferred to take some game bird feathers with me when I go to see the litter. Ideally, I like to schedule my visit for a time when the puppies will be outside in the yard playing. I then stand upwind of the playing puppies and wave the feathers behind my back – out of sight to the pups. The first puppy that gets a whiff of the scent and comes to investigate is the one I choose. I can't guarantee that this method is any better than others – but it has always worked out well for me.

Other experienced dog folks advocate letting the puppy choose you – and picking the first pup that comes over to greet you. Still others depend upon puppy personality tests – though I have to admit to a great deal of skepticism about these tests. Finally, some advocate looking for certain colors (the German hunters of olden times used to believe that solid liver females made the best brood bitches – and my own experience is in line with their beliefs), or physical traits. As noted above, if you have chosen a good litter – all of these methods are likely to work. Use the one in which you have the most faith.

MALE OR FEMALE?

German Shorthairs have a set of dentures a Doberman would envy.

One of the questions that new owners often ask is whether they should pick a male or female pup? Typically, breeders will charge slightly more for a female pup than they will for a male because a female can have litters that over a lifetime will generate substantially more income than a typical male's stud fees. On the other hand, many owners are turned off by the thought of a female coming into season twice per year.

The truth is that each of the sexes has their pros and cons. Out of a good litter, both should make fine hunting dogs – so it really comes down to a matter of preference.

My experience with German Shorthair females has been that they generally tend to come on at a slightly earlier age than the males. There are exceptions of course, but as a general rule female pups seem to learn their lessons a bit quicker than the males. Females will often be pointing and retrieving well at five or six months of age – while their brothers may take a couple of months longer to get to the same level of proficiency. Females don't tend to be as rambunctious and easily distracted in puppyhood –and as a consequence they typically pay better attention to their training and their lessons afield. If I had to describe this characteristic, I would say that it is a matter of focus. Females tend to have better focus at a younger age, while males tend to be a bit more scattered in their attention at the same age. Having said this, the males catch up quickly and by the second year there is rarely any difference in terms of focus or hunting proficiency.

Physically, where German Shorthairs are concerned, females are smaller and more lightly built than the males. This has an impact on the way they tend to hunt. Females in general don't tend to be as physical as males in terms of charging into thick brush and through obstacles. Quite often they will puzzle out a way to search the brush thoroughly with their nose without busting their way through it the way a male would.

This should not, however, be taken as an indication that females aren't as tough or aggressive as the males in their own way. I believe that females tend to be a bit more protective of the home and family – and are better as watchdogs at barking and alerting the family to potential threats. I would also say that anyone who looks at the teeth on a German Shorthair will have nothing but respect for the damage the breed can inflict should it decide to do so. After all, they are bred to kill foxes, badgers and other "vermin". They have a set of dentures that a Doberman would envy. I would not want to tangle with a female German Shorthair protecting the family children or dealing with an intruder in the house. On the down side, when German Shorthair females don't get along with other female dogs – the fights in my experience are almost always much more fierce than the males. It seems to me that the males tend to fight to prove something – and typically stop once that's been settled. The females tend to fight for good. German Shorthair females are typically sweet, loving dogs – but at the same time they are also often tough broads who take no guff. If you have an older female dog at home who is an alpha – I'd think twice about bringing home a younger GSP female.

As for the issue of a female coming into season – I think the inconvenience is a bit overstated. Typically, females will come into season twice per year – with the heat lasting two to three weeks. A pair of the appropriate sized panties and sanitary napkins will take care of the problems associated with spotting – and keeping the girl inside when not under direct supervision and physically separated from male dogs will take care of the potential for unwanted pregnancies. I have never considered this minor inconvenience of the canine female reproductive cycle to be much of a problem.

As a general rule, as noted above male German Shorthairs tend to lack the early focus of the females. While, again, there are some notable exceptions, I think they also tend to develop physically a bit more slowly –holding on to that gangly legs and big puppy feet stage a little longer. As a consequence, in my experience males typically tend to be less effective in the field than their female counterparts until they reach about 7 months to a year of age. At this age they have developed physically to the point that they have grown into their body. This makes them more effective hunters and I think this also tends to concentrate their focus a bit.

While males don't go into heat like females, they also have their reproductive challenges. The two most notable are marking and fighting. Housebreaking and training can teach males not to lift their legs on furniture or other items in the house – but when a female goes into season, or a rival male is introduced into the household, the training often gets temporarily forgotten. In such circumstances, you will have to use extra vigilance that you wouldn't with a female. As for fighting, most males are not extremely pugnacious. In general, the German Shorthair temperament is one that doesn't tend to start fights – but does tend to finish them. Males on the same level in the social hierarchy pose the greatest threat for fights - though generally only when there are also territorial considerations involved. In a neutral territory, like the hunting field, most German Shorthair males will be fine with other dogs as long as those dogs aren't aggressive.

Males are typically about ten percent taller and twenty percent heavier than females. This extra height and weight gives them extra physical capabilities that tends to influence the hunting style of males. As noted before, where females will often try to negotiate their way through thick cover – or even shy away – males will generally plunge in. One clear example I can point to concerns catclaw, a plant I've described elsewhere. quail love to hide in catclaw because so few predators will risk the lacerations to get to them. My females tend to be a bit reluctant to work in catclaw, and when they do they try and negotiate their way around individual bushes and avoid the thorns. My males tend to plunge in with little regard for the thorns. When my males come out of a catclaw thicket, I typically have to apply styptic pencil to small cuts on ears and noses – or cold water to rinse off the nick on a tongue. They don't seem bothered at all. The females rarely have the cuts, but they also work the thickets much more slowly and less thoroughly.

I think the physicality also shows up on waterfowl. While both sexes have little difficulty retrieving wounded ducks – some differences show up when it comes to geese and larger waterfowl. A wounded gander can be intimidating for any dog – and is probably one of the more difficult retrieves in the waterfowl world. My males, which tend to be towards the top end of the breed standard when it comes to size, will generally run at the gander and bowl it over, get a good grip, and then retrieve it. The females don't tend to bowl over the gander, but rather run and circle it until they see an opportunity to lunge in and get a good grip. Both methods are effective in that they result in a retrieved bird – but they illustrate a small difference in the way the two sexes tend to go about their business.

Finally, I think that the difference in physical size also has an effect on personality. Both sexes of German Shorthairs are affectionate and strongly loyal. However, the social interaction seems to me to be subtly different between myself and dogs of each sex. My females have been a bit more prone to trying manipulation for want of a better word. They seem a bit more adept at playing on my emotions to get what they want, and a bit more covert in undertaking activities that they know would not find favor with me. Most of this comes under the heading of things that just make you smile or laugh at how well they have you trained. Sometimes it can result in downright sneakiness. Males tend to be a bit more emotionally transparent –their likes and dislikes seem to me a bit more obvious. They also don't seem to be as adept at manipulation – and I think in general they tend to be a bit more straightforward. Both sexes are, however, equally as good at provoking smiles and chuckles.

German Shorthair litters often have a variety of coat patterns. This litter had pups with solid liver, liver tick, roan, and white with liver patch coats.

COLOR

Coat color is an important consideration for a hunting dog – and the German Shorthair coat with it's variations of Liver and White (and Black in the non-US versions) offers a wide selection for the hunter. The German Shorthair coat is broken into five basic coat color patterns:

Liver ticked:

This is the most common Shorthair coat pattern and the one by which the breed is best known. This coat is a mix of white and liver guard hairs, with liver colored hair predominant. The underfur is liver as well. Often this coat combination will include liver patches –and typically the head is liver as well. This is probably the most utilitarian of the Shorthair coat colors where the hunter is concerned. The ticking pattern of this coat offers the German Shorthair natural camouflage that serves it well in the duck blind –and helps it avoid spooking game in the field.

76

At the same time, the white element of the coat helps to keep the coat relatively cool in bright, warm conditions. It is all around probably the most versatile of the GSP coat patterns – as well as being the most common. It can be a difficult coat to see in uplands at times, but with a bright colored collar this problem is largely mitigated.

Roan:

Roan is a variation of the ticked pattern in which white hairs predominate over liver colored hairs. The underfur is often liver, though I've seen some roan dogs with an underfur that seems almost cream in color. The roan Shorthair is a light colored dog with ticking patterns that appear much fainter than the standard liver ticked –almost faded. The overall impression is of a dog with a whitish coat with light grey or light brown ticking. Such dogs do not have liver patches on their body. Again, the head on such roan dogs is typically liver in color. It's hard to know how common the true roan coloration is because it is usually treated as simply a variant of the liver ticked coat. From my own experience, I would say that probably 15% of the pups I've produced over the years were true Roans – slightly less than the solid liver coloration in my line. Roan makes a very heat resistant coat – and these dogs tend to run cool in bright, warm conditions. They are particularly popular for hunting desert quail – though their coat color does tend to be extremely visible when hunting waterfowl.

Roan dogs can have either pink or dark pads on their feet. This is another important consideration because in my experience pink pads tend to be significantly more tender and prone to injury than dark pads. If you are hunting rugged country such as the chukar country of the Great Basin, or the Gambel's country of the southwest – dogs with dark padded feet will be easier to maintain. If you are hunting primarily in forest, on grass or gravel, or agricultural fields – then pad color isn't as much of an issue.

German hunters in past times believed that solid liver bitches made the best dams for breeding hunting dogs.

Solid Liver:

This is just what the description indicates – a coat that is solid liver in coloration. Often these coats have a small white patch on chest, or some white ticking on the feet. Some of the greatest of the early German Shorthairs had this coat, and it became a favorite of some of the early German hunters. It was the stated belief of many of the old German breeders that solid liver bitches tended to throw exceptionally good hunting dogs – and while I'm not sure about the science I will say that my practical experience has been that this is true. All of the solid liver bitches I've owned have been good hunters and produced great hunting litters.

This tends to be a warm coat that absorbs a lot of passive solar radiation. The solid liver bitches that I've used for hunting Gambel's quail in the southwest have all felt the heat a bit more than their ticked coat offspring and I had to take care to rest them and water them a little more. Having said that, I never had one case of heat exhaustion – so solid liver Shorthairs shouldn't be automatically eliminated for warm weather upland hunting. In some respects liver has visibility issues as well. Certainly a solid liver dog working the uplands is more visible than a ticked GSP. However, I don't think that they have as much of a visibility problem when it comes to waterfowl as the roan and white coated Shorthairs do. Solid liver Shorthairs all have dark pads.

White-liver patched (Pointer colored):

As the description indicates, this coat has both white and liver colored hair in a pattern that does not intermingle. The Germans call this coat "Klar" or clear. Essentially this is a solid white coat with patches, where they exist, of solid liver. These dogs typically have solid liver heads. This was never a popular coat color with the Germans because of its extreme visibility and because it tends to have more sparse underfur that makes it less suitable for cold water work. Less than 1% of German Shorthairs typically have this coat coloration in Germany.

It is for this reason that the coat color has become fraught with so much controversy here in the United States. The Pointer colored coat is extremely common among field trial strains of German Shorthairs. As an estimate, I would guess that roughly 20 percent of American Shorthairs now have this coat coloration. It's prevalence among field trial strains of Shorthairs, combined with strong rumors of field trialers crossbreeding to Pointers have led many to believe that German Shorthairs sporting such coats are automatically mixed breeds. While such coats would provide cover for such crossbreeding – at the same time this is a naturally occurring coat color that has a long history with the breed.

To a degree the popularity of this coat coloration can be attributed to hunters in the southern tier of the US who prefer a white coat for its visibility and its heat reflecting qualities in warm conditions. (This is why I tend to give Shorthairs that sport a Pointer colored coat the benefit of the doubt unless I see other Pointer conformation characteristics such as a clear stop, a dish face, a Pointer chest, or a Pointer butt.) Whether this preference alone, rather than significant crossbreeding, is enough to account for the abnormally high prevalence of this coat color in field trial Shorthairs is doubtful.

Black ticked:

In all of the countries outside of the US black is also an accepted German Shorthair coloration. While those with black ticked coats are still a small percentage of the German Shorthair population – some notable Deutsch Kurzhaars of recent times have been black coated. Black ticked gives the color combination that is often called "blue ticked" among hounds. It is a rare coat color in the US because black is not an accepted color in the US breed standard, and GSPs sporting this coat are not eligible to participate in AKC competitions. As you would expect, a black ticked coat tends to be a warm coat that easily absorbs passive solar radiation from the sun.

Solid Black:

This is perhaps the most uncommon coat color of them all. Solid black is, as its name implies a coat consisting of solid black hairs. As with solid liver dogs, a patch of white on the chest or some white ticking on the feet is often present. This is the hottest of German Shorthair coats and would be of limited utility for upland hunting in warm climates.

One final note about German Shorthair coats is that puppies' coats darken as they get older. The pup that you think might have a roan coat because of the faint ticking at six weeks of age, will generally turn out to be a clearly liver ticked dog at six months. A rule of thumb is to assume that the coat will be twice as dark as it appears at six weeks. Pad color will remain the same – the dark or pink padded pup will also have the same colored pads as an adult.

AMERICAN FIELD TRIALS AND HUNTING DOGS

This is perhaps a good time to talk a bit about field trials and breeders who specialize in breeding field trial dogs. I have previously been critical of the impact that field trialers have had upon the German Shorthair in America –and this is a good place to explain the reason for that criticism.

Americans have an almost mystical reverence for competition. From our youngest years, we are socialized by our culture to admire winners in everything from football to spelling bees. So when it comes to picking a hunting dog – many hunters are immediately entranced by the fact that one or more of the pup's parents are "Champions." They immediately think of this as something positive, something to value – and the big professional breeders know this. Many big kennels prominently advertize the field trial titles their dogs have, and speak of non-titled dogs as "unproven" or worse. Hunters often fall for this – many times to their great regret. They like the idea of being able to brag that their dog comes from "championship stock." Those hunters who might be new to the world of hunting dogs, or unsure of their judgment and knowledge when it comes to hunting dogs, also like the idea that a dog has supposedly been "judged" by "experts." As a result, many fine Shorthair breeders who have little interest in participating in field trials and recognize their limitations have told me that they have no choice but to title their dogs – it's what the market wants.

The problem is that most hunters don't understand what field trials are and how they are judged. They think that they are hunting contests, and the winner is the best hunter. While there are trial formats that try to broadly imitate hunting situations and to judge dogs on how they find, point, and retrieve birds – the classic trial formats don't. Instead, these are formalized contests in which handlers and spectators are mounted on horseback in order to keep up with the huge running dogs they campaign. These trials have little or nothing to do with the type of hunting most Americans do –and not surprisingly tend to produce dogs that are inferior hunting dogs.

The traditional field trials run by the American Kennel Club and the American Field (Field Dog Stud Book) are divided into two basic types:.

All Age trials are focused on rewarding dogs that run very far, very fast. The dogs are judged on their independence, the length and speed of the casts they make, and how they look on point if they find a bird. The aesthetics of what field trialers call "style and class" are what concerns All Age judges – not their bird finding ability. All Age dogs are not judged on how many birds they find or point, and as birds are not shot during these trials they are not judged on their ability to retrieve. Very little of what goes in to making an All Age champion is directly transferable to foot hunting – and while field trialers often claim that their All Age dogs can make fine foot hunting dogs- I've never seen one that actually did. In general they tend to be self hunting run offs that miss a lot of birds. I've hunted over the years with dozens of hunting dogs from the top All Age stock and my dogs have never failed to find, point and retrieve more birds – not once. While it may say something about the quality of my German Shorthairs, I believe it also speaks volumes about the hunting abilities of All Age dogs.

Gun Dog or Shooting Dog stakes are, according to their rules, focused on producing more moderate ranged and paced dogs with characteristics that should make them good hunting dogs. In the past, the majority of German Shorthair champions were from this type of trial – and it has to be admitted that some outstanding hunters came from Gun Dog stock. During my time with German Shorthairs I've seen a number of fine hunters come from Gun Dog stakes (or Shooting Dog stakes in the American Field vernacular).

Unfortunately, I think this is a declining trend. Over the years many field trial judges have come to focus on the range and speed of gun dog and shooting dog participants at the expense of the other important hunting characteristics. They often judge these stakes as though they are simply mini-All Age stakes. It is not unusual nowadays to find dogs that have earned championships in both All Age and Gun Dog stakes, although according to the printed rules these are two almost diametrically different types of dogs. What this means is that while it is still theoretically possible to find decent hunting dogs coming from Gun Dog field trial stock – in practice it is very difficult and getting more difficult to do so each year. All in all, my advice would be to stay away from anyone focused on breeding and competing in horseback trials if you want to find a quality hunting pup. Your odds of finding a quality hunting pup are much better looking elsewhere.

Having said that - disenchantment with the artificiality of horseback trials has led over the last few decades to the rise of a number of types of walking field trial formats that more closely mimic hunting. The best known of these is NSTRA, or the National Shoot To Retrieve Association. NSTRA trials are run on smaller fields in which birds have been stocked. Two dogs are run on each field at one time. The dogs are followed and handled by gunners who flush and shoot the birds that each dog finds and points. The dogs are awarded points for the number of birds found and pointed, for backing, for retrieving, for their run, and for how they handle. The focus of NSTRA was to provide a format in which hunters could compete with their dogs in the off season – and to provide a field trial venue focused on producing hunting dogs. Unfortunately, the competitive spirit has driven some clubs out west and in the south to enlarge their trial grounds, and to start awarding extra points to dogs that run far and fast. Whereas it used to be a given that German Shorthairs competing successfully in NSTRA were likely to make fine hunting dogs –that is no longer always the case. There are now some German Shorthairs competing in NSTRA that would be more at home in a horseback field trial. Those looking to get a hunting pup from NSTRA German Shorthairs should see the parents hunt before committing –and should avoid those that seem to have more run than hunt.

A number of other trial formats have also been started in recent years that have hunters on foot, and which have birds shot and retrieved as part of the trial. Even the AKC and the American Field have been increasing the number of walking stakes that they hold. While this is arguably a step in the right direction where the German Shorthairs (and the other continental breeds) are concerned - a hunter still needs to be skeptical of the claims of field trial breeders that their stock will make outstanding hunters simply because they are field trialed. As pointed out above – there is tremendous variety in field trial formats and the characteristics on which champions are chosen in the various formats. Anyone seeking a good hunting pup needs to understand this, and understand the characteristics of the various trials, so they can accurately assess the impact of field trial champions on the line they are looking at. An All Age champion will be a very different dog with very different characteristics from a NSTRA champion – and their impacts on a blood line will be radically different.

The rule of thumb for hunters who insist upon field trial blood is that the field trial format that most closely imitates the type of hunting that you intend to do is the one that is most likely to have breeders producing pups capable of doing the type of hunting you want to do. Also, the trial format that doesn't award prizes based first and foremost upon finding and pointing birds is largely worthless where a hunter is concerned. Finally, remember that field trial titles are never a substitute for hunting credentials. If you want to see some champions in your dog's pedigree, try to make sure that those titles were earned in trial formats that most closely imitate your type of hunting –and that the parents are the kind of hunters you would like to own.

5

Bringing Your Pup Home

Ideally, you will have a couple of weeks between the time you pick a pup, and the time it is ready to come home with you. This will give you some time to make preparations for the new arrival. You want to make sure that you have a safe, loving environment prepared for the puppy. Your puppy will need its own food dish and a water dish. These need to have low sides so that a small puppy can eat and drink out of them. Because the puppy will outgrow these dishes in a couple of months, I tend to use an inexpensive enameled steel pie tin for the food dish – and a suitable flat bottomed bowl for the water dish. (When the puppy grows large enough for big dog utensils, I prefer a large stainless steel feeding bowl and water dish.) Unfortunately, if you use a pie tin for water it will typically become a puppy wading pool with German Shorthairs. It's best to find a flat bottomed bowl heavy enough to avoid being tipped over and small enough not to make an inviting puppy pool.

A word of advice about feeding and drinking bowls – avoid plastic. Plastic releases chemicals in a process called outgassing to which many dogs are sensitive. In fact, there is a malady called "collie nose" in which the dog's sensitive nasal tissue gets raw and ulcerated from exposure to the chemicals in plastic. Instead of purchasing plastic dishes, make sure that your dog's eating and drinking bowls are made from metal or crockery (without lead based glaze) that are pet safe.

Your pup will also need a comfortable place to sleep. For the first week or so, I typically let the pup sleep at night in a cardboard box lined with newspaper that is tall enough to keep the puppy from crawling out. I put in old folded towels and bedding to keep the pup comfortable and warm – and perhaps a favorite puppy toy or two. After the pup is capable of climbing out of the box on its own - which usually happens earlier than I want or expect – I move the puppy to a puppy crate. Even though the puppy will soon outgrow this crate – I want the first crate to be small enough to give the puppy a sense of security in its "den." I line the crate with newspaper because small puppies don't always have control over their bladders or bowels no matter how hard they try – and there will be the occasional accident. Paper makes dealing with these messes pretty easy.

Paper also provides traction for the pup –which is an important consideration for puppies whose musculoskeletal systems are still forming. Puppies can have real problems getting traction on slippery floors – which can result in injuries and problems that may affect their future development. Where possible – try and keep young puppies off of slippery floors and on surfaces that provide them traction.

Avoid any of the bedding materials that contain cedar chips or other types of cedar products. These materials are advertised as having insecticidal properties that will repel or kill ticks and fleas. While cedar does indeed have chemicals that will kill insects, the same chemicals are also toxic to dogs – and humans. They irritate nasal membranes and respiratory systems –and in large doses such as occur at sawmills have been found to cause severe illness and death in humans. Hunting dogs depend so much upon their noses for success in the field that any bedding that contains a chemical that is likely to irritate nasal membranes should be avoided.

You also want to use this time to find a good veterinarian. Your puppy will need vaccinations and examinations shortly after you take it home –so having a good vet in which you have confidence lined up beforehand will make this all easier. If you already have a vet that you like, then you only have to worry about scheduling appointments for the pup to be examined and receive its puppy vaccinations. If you don't have a good veterinarian – ask the breeder and/or other experienced hunting dog owners for references. Since hunting dogs have health issues that are different and often more complicated than dogs that are simply pets, having a vet with experience with hunting dogs is a major advantage.

The profession of veterinary medicine is in a state of flux in the United States as this book is written. A good portion of the profession wants to see veterinary medicine work much more like human medicine in the United States. These veterinarians are seeking salaries comparable to those of human doctors, and routinely use some of the very expensive high tech equipment and treatments that are used by human physicians. While these veterinarians have some good arguments for why they should be paid the same as physicians, and why they should have offices with MRI machines and other very expensive equipment – there is also a significant downside to this trend.

The model for providing human medicine in the United States is widely criticized as being exceptionally expensive and unacceptably elitist. By all international evaluations, it doesn't do a very good job of providing quality health care to the vast majority of citizens. Having veterinary medicine imitate this system, with all of its flaws, has the potential to price treatment out of the reach of most animal owners, and lower the overall quality of animal care in the US.

On the other hand, there is still a sizeable number of veterinarians who are rejecting this trend, and who want to see veterinary medicine move toward an improved and more profitable model of the traditional sole practitioner. These vets do not want to be part of the larger clinics necessary to afford expensive high tech equipment, and instead use methods that are less high tech, but more focused on the skill and knowledge of the practitioner –and quality of care. My own recommendation is that you find a veterinarian in the latter class – and avoid large clinics and emergency vet hospitals. A good, knowledgeable vet who cares about your dog and who is willing to discuss treatment with you, and who's prices are reasonable– is a far better choice than a clinic with all of the fancy equipment, but impersonal care, and pricing that makes you wonder if you can afford to give your dog the care it needs.

VACCINATIONS AND WORMING

All puppies should receive their vaccinations and be wormed. Until about five weeks of age, most puppies are protected by their mother's antibodies that they receive from the colostrum in their mother's milk. The length of time this protection lasts varies from puppy to puppy. This protection can interfere with the effectiveness of the vaccines – so we typically give puppies an initial vaccination at around six weeks of age, and then three booster vaccinations spaced about three weeks apart to ensure that every pup gets the immunity conferred by vaccinations.

Depending upon the advice of your veterinarian – your pup will be given either a 5 way or a 7 way vaccine. The five way vaccine inoculates the puppy against canine distemper, hepatitis, adenovirus cough, parainfluenza, and parvovirus. The seven way inoculates the puppy against the diseases above, with the addition of two forms of inoculation against leptospirosis. Depending upon where you live, the vaccinations against leptospirosis may not be needed. Your puppy should also receive its first rabies vaccination at around 12 weeks of age.

Most puppies are infected with worms by their mother at an early age. They should be wormed by the breeder at four, and six weeks of age – and you should continue worming every two weeks for another month. Be sure to make sure that whatever worming medication you are using is safe for puppies, and to follow the dosing instructions carefully.

AT WHAT AGE SHOULD I PICK UP THE PUP?

Animal behaviorists have come up with a number of theories about the phases of a dog's psychological development and the optimal time a puppy should be separated from the litter. Unfortunately, given the imprecise nature of such research – they have come up with some widely differing views on the subject. The traditional view is that pups are best separated from the litter between seven and eight weeks of age. Some behaviorists say that 13 weeks is the optimal time. Personally, I'm not sure that it really matters that much. I've always picked up my pups between seven and eight weeks – and they've always turned out to be fine hunters and companions. When I breed a litter, I send the pups home with their owners at that age as well.

I like to send pups home at around seven to eight weeks because I like to see my pups start their training at an early age. I also think that pups around that age tend to bond more tightly with their owners, which again makes training easier.

At six weeks, these young pups are just about ready to leave the litter and go home with their new owners.

While I'm not sure that waiting an additional month makes a significant difference in terms of training and bonding – I do believe that waiting much longer than that can have an impact on the type of training I prefer to do. I therefore recommend that those picking up a pup try and do so within that seven to eight week window if possible, but not to fight with the breeder if they prefer to wait until 13 weeks.

For those who get started dogs, or who rescue older dogs, the nature of the training and bonding process is somewhat different –and I will discuss some of those issues later on. This section, however, will focus on those who are bringing home a young pup.

THE FIRST DAY

For a puppy, that first day of going to a new home is traumatic. For the first time in its life it is separated from it's dam, and from its littermates. From this point forward, its whole life will be different. As a social animal – the feeling of loneliness can be terrifying. It is up to you to provide a nurturing environment and sense of belonging to help the pup overcome it's fright. It's also up to you to provide plenty of understanding and empathy.

Friday is probably the optimal day to pick up a pup if you are going to have the following weekend relatively free. The reason is that your new pup is likely going to take some time to get acclimated to the new surroundings, and its new family. The first night is almost inevitably going to involve a fair amount of crying unless you have an older dog that is willing to snuggle and comfort the pup. The pup is frightened, lonely, and lost – you'd cry too if you were in that situation. It's therefore best to be prepared for some sleep deprivation for the first night or two.

Many of the classic dog books have a variety of recommendations for helping the pup get through these first nights. Some recommend a hot water bottle to imitate the warmth of the dam and litter, others recommend a stuffed animal to simulate a sibling, and still others talk of putting a mechanical alarm clock under the bedding so that the regular ticking will remind the pup of the heartbeat of its littermates. I think there is some value in all of these tricks – but none is sufficient to overcome the loneliness a pup will feel on that first night. This is why I let the pup sleep in a cardboard box right next to my bed. The water bottle, the stuffed animal, and comfortable bedding will help the puppy fall asleep. However the best comfort for a new pup in the middle of the night is your loving hand.

When the pup begins to fuss and cry – I try and sooth it with calming words in a quiet tone. When that doesn't work, I roll over and reach into the box to stroke and comfort the pup. Generally, the mere presence of a warm, living hand is enough to get the pup to settle down and go back to sleep. What the pup wants most in the world is to know that it is not alone, but is rather part of a pack that will love and take care of it.

HOUSEBREAKING

Young pups, like infants, lack the bladder size and development to sleep a full eight hours without going to the bathroom. Your pup will have accidents –and you need to be prepared for this. This is much less of an issue nowadays then it was before the advent of steam cleaners and effective spot removers, and I recommend that new puppy owners purchase both. A steam cleaner can fully and effectively clean up messes from carpet – limiting the dire consequences of puppy

Puppies are an investment in the future – a bet that if played right will pay off with years filled with priceless days afield

accidents. For older soiling that you find by accident – there are spot removers that are remarkably effective at making such things disappear. The one that I have found most effective is marketed in the United States under the brand name Folex – and is found in many grocery stores. I recommend avoiding old fashioned spot removers that leave a residue that needs to be vacuumed – I haven't found these to work very well.

The most important thing to remember is that you need to use common sense with your new arrival, and you need to be tolerant. Don't let the pup onto valuable carpets or into areas where a puppy accident will be a crisis. When such accidents do occur, scold the puppy only if you catch it in the act. Then, without harshness, take it immediately outside to finish its business. Do NOT spank the puppy, or hit it with a rolled up newspaper, or rub its nose in it. These things will only make the puppy fearful of you – and will have as much effect as if you did the same thing to a six month old infant. What you are trying to do is let the pup know the boundaries of where it is not all right to relieve itself, and where it is all right to do so.

A puppies natural instinct is to keep its den area clean. In the wild, once pups can leave the den, they poop and pee away from the den. This keeps predators from locating the den by its smell, and perhaps having a puppy dinner. This is a very fundamental, primitive instinct that almost all German Shorthair pups have. Housetraining uses this basic instinct to teach the pup not to go in the house.

The secret to helping the pup learn this is to start with a small "den" area, and then enlarge that eventually to encompass the whole house. The cardboard box is the first step in this process. We don't want a large box because we want the puppy to identify it as a den. However, recognizing that the pup is going to have accidents – we need to give it an acceptable emergency backup. This is why I first line the cardboard box (perhaps twenty inches by thirty inches) with newspaper. I then put in bedding in one corner of the box along with whatever toys I want the pup to have. I leave the area opposite the bedding clear of everything except newspapers. What you will typically find is that the puppy will leave its bedding to poop and pee in the opposite corner.

If the pup whines, or otherwise lets you know that it needs to go out – you need to take the pup outside. It doesn't matter if its snowing, or if its 4:00am – you want to encourage the pup not relieving itself in its den, and letting you know when it has to go outside. Once you get to this point, you are halfway through the battle.

Once the pup is sleeping through the night – usually after a few days – I then transfer the pup and its bedding to a puppy crate. I typically set up the crate the same way that I set up the cardboard box: bedding in the back, open newspaper in the front. While the crate doesn't have to sit right next to the bed as I recommend for the cardboard box – it should still be in the bedroom where the pup can sense, see and hear other members of the pack sleeping all night. At first the pup may squawk and squall -but as long as it has learned to sleep comfortably in close proximity to you it should settle down.

The reason we close the pup into a crate at night is that if the door is left open the pup will leave its "den" and poop and pee outside the crate – on your carpet. It is important that you take the pup out to pee and poop as close as possible to being closed in for the night – and that you stay outside and watch the pup until it goes (this may take some time as the pup dithers and explores its surroundings). It is best that you do so in a closed in area –such as a fenced back yard, where the pup will be regularly allowed out to relieve itself. The closed in area will limit the pup's ability to run off and play –and because dogs are very place conscious, the regular trip to the same area will encourage the pup to go. Once the pup is sleeping in its crate without accidents, then you can leave the door open at night if you want.

One of the keys to avoiding accidents during the waking hours is taking the pup out regularly to relieve itself. Remembering that the pup has a bladder the size of a walnut, taking the pup out for a walk or run every two hours or so should help it avoid accidents in the house –and get in the habit of going outside. Also, learn to read your pup's body language. Often the puppy will get a bit anxious and start sniffing the ground when it has to go out. When the pup does go to the bathroom outside – make sure to praise it when it does. We are thus letting the pup know that going outside is a good thing.

Two things to be noted about crates. The first is that a crate is NOT punishment. It is a substitute den for the dog – one where the dog should feel comfortable and safe. Do NOT use the crate as punishment for young puppies – nor as a substitute for keeping an eye on the pup as it plays. You might want to keep the puppy's bedding in the crate with the door open during the day – so the pup can go in and out as it pleases. Ideally, you want the pup to feel comfortable enough in the crate to take naps in it. The second thing to note is that you will need to buy two crates for your dog. The first, puppy crate needs to be small enough to give the pup a feeling of security – like a womb. While it should be large enough to let the puppy turn around and stand up with ease – it should also be cozy. Small or medium sized crates are typically the best sizes for GSP pups. However, your pup will outgrow that puppy crate within a few months. At that point, I recommend switching the pup to an adult, Large or preferably Extra Large crate. This will be the dog's crate for the rest of its life.

I know some dog owners who swear by wire cages – but I prefer the plastic crates. They have a number of advantages over wire cages. The first is that with solid bottoms and tops and ventilated sides –they give that feeling of being enclosed so central to the concept of a den. To get that with wire cages you need to cover the cages. The second advantage they have is that the solid plastic bottom of a crate will contain any messes from leaking onto the floor, and can be easily cleaned with a hose and some soap and water. Finally, I think the crates are safer for transporting the dogs. Most airlines won't accept wire cages for shipping.

Ideally, it is best to have some daytime supervision for a young pup. They are curious and ignorant of the consequences of their actions –which is a recipe for mischief. They also have a strong urge to teethe, and to put things in their mouth. If the pup is to be left alone for short periods of time, it can be put into its crate. Again, the crate is not a place of punishment, but a safe "den" that is uniquely the pup's. The pup should look forward to spending some time in the crate. If you have to use some treats to help reinforce this view, then don't hesitate to do so.

If you don't have the option of staying home with the young pup – then ideally you need to set up a safe area where the pup can sleep and play during the daytime. One option that is commonly used is to get a "puppy gate" and seal off part of the kitchen in which the pup can stay for the day. The kitchen is often the room of choice because it typically has flooring that is easy to clean and which will not be damaged by puppy accidents or spills. Inside of the puppy play area put down a food and water dish for the pup (take care to make sure the pup has access to clean, cool water during the day). Also put down some bedding for the pup (though nothing that can be easily shredded). You also want to put in some toys for the pup, and particularly shank bones and other things on which the pup can safely chew and teethe. Finally, put down some newspapers for the pup at the opposite end of the room from the bedding and food dishes. Don't paper the whole area because you want to get the puppy to identify the newspapers as a specific place where it is acceptable to go – and if the whole area is covered with newspapers then the pup won't be able to spot any difference

FEEDING YOUR PUP

When your pup comes home it should have been successfully weaned and be comfortable eating solid food on its own. Start the pup off with the puppy food used by the breeder. If it is a good quality food and the pup likes it – then you may want to stay with it. If it is an inexpensive, lower quality puppy food then you should switch the pup over to a good quality food. Do so gradually to avoid digestive upsets by mixing a small amount of the new food with the old, and gradually increasing the amount until the switch has been made. I like to mix dry puppy food with a bit of canned puppy food, or some cottage cheese, and some hot water to make an appetizing "stew." I carefully follow the recommended amounts on the food package for the size of the pup.

Young pups have small stomachs but enormous metabolisms. They are converting food and nutrients into muscle and bone at an amazing rate. You can actually see them grow from week to week (and perhaps even day to day). This means that they need to be fed at regular intervals throughout the course of the day. Young pups should be fed four times per day at regular intervals. German Shorthair pups are typically not finicky eaters. They generally attack their food. Try not to give the pup its last meal any later than 8:00 pm in order to allow it to poop before it goes to bed. Late feeding and watering is putting the pup under unnecessary pressure to hold it in overnight.

In any breed there are some pups that prefer play to eating, or which have different tastes for different foods. These pups will often ignore their food, or only eat a few bites and then turn their attention elsewhere. With such puppies, I make it a practice to pick up the bowl after about 15 minutes. This encourages the pup to finish the food it is fed, and prevents the pup from using its food as a toy to be scattered or rolled in. It also helps you monitor how much the pup is actually eating. If the pup really appears to be off of its feed, have it checked out by the vet as soon as possible. There are a variety of ailments that can put pups off their feed -and if untreated many can turn out to be quite serious.

I typically move from a four times per day feeding schedule to a three times per day schedule when the pup is around four months old. I then move to a two times per day schedule when the pup hits six months –and then a one time per day schedule at around ten months of age. At six months, I switch the pup from puppy food to a high quality adult dog food – again I like to feed my dogs a mixture of dry food, canned food, and hot water. I believe that this kind of "stew" helps avoid gastric torsion (bloat).

Bloat is a life threatening situation where the dog's stomach twists and pinches it off from the intestines. As a consequence, digesting food releases methane, which causes the dog's abdomen to swell. If the pressure is not relieved immediately it can do damage to the dog's organs, and if the blood supply to the intestines is not restored it can lead to gangrene and death. We don't really understand what causes bloat – it used to be thought that too much activity after eating, or drinking too much water after eating a large amount of dry food, were the primary causes of bloat in deep chested dogs such as German Shorthairs. Science has not been able to confirm those beliefs. We don't really know what causes bloat. However, I do know that in thirty five years of feeding my dogs as described – I've never had a case of bloat. While this is only anecdotal evidence, I do feel that although this is not scientific, it is at least an anecdote worth passing on.

TEETHING

One of the rules of dogdom is that puppies chew on things. They chew because they are teething, and their puppy teeth are being replaced by adult teeth. Chewing helps ease the discomfort of that transition. They also chew because like small children, one of the ways they explore their world is by putting everything in their mouth. It is also a great way for a pup to work off extra energy or anxiety.

This means that we have to have plenty of things for our young pup to chew on. One of the rules of puppydom is that if you don't have things that you want your puppy to chew on, your puppy will chew on things that you don't want them to chew on – shoes, electrical cords, furniture, etc. It's a pretty simple choice.

There is a huge industry devoted to making things for puppies and dogs to chew on. In my experience the majority of these are a waste of money where German Shorthairs are concerned. Either puppies have no interest in chewing on them, or they reduce them to shreds in a very short time. Some of the inexpensive plastic toys are actually dangerous in that pieces can block a pup's intestines and cause a medical emergency. Over the years I've come to rely on a few old standards when it comes to helping puppies with chewing.

The first of these is the cattle shank bone. You can buy these in many super markets that sell them as soup bones. I try and find shank bones about three to four inches long –and then boil them in salt water. I first give them to the pup outside, or on some safe surface where the marrow, and the meat and gristle remaining on the bone won't stain my carpets. Within a half hour the pup will have gnawed off all of the extraneous material – leaving a polished bone with walls thick enough that even a Shorthair can't splinter it. Such a bone will last for months – and it's great for puppies working on new teeth. It's also an excellent tool for keeping adult dogs teeth in good shape – so I continue giving my dogs shank bones throughout their lives.

The second of these is a length of knotted rope. This is particularly good for young puppies that are getting rid of their milk teeth. The fibers massage sore gums and allow a pup to really sink its teeth into something. The only bad part about the rope is that when it gets dragged into the yard (as it will if it isn't closely monitored) it becomes a mop and picks up mud, slime, weed seeds, and other stuff that is best left outside. Some versions also have a tendency to shed fibers that wind up everywhere. On the positive side, some of the nylon versions can be put in the washing machine when they get too disgusting – extending their useful life.

Providing puppies with things upon which to chew is essential for their health, and your peace of mind.

The third of these is rawhide in either the bone, roll, or chip form. German Shorthairs love any of them. Rawhide is somewhat controversial in that it can reportedly cause intestinal blockages in some dogs, and cheap foreign imports can sometimes have harmful chemicals. However, I've never had a problem with a German Shorthair getting an intestinal blockage (though plenty have thrown up some chewed rawhide), and I make sure to buy quality rawhide from reputable sources.

The final one is the venerable ball. I buy both tennis balls, and the hard rubber balls. The tennis balls give the pup loads of fun – though it doesn't take them long to pop them. Once a tennis ball has been punctured or torn – it should be removed from the pup. Otherwise the pup will tear it into small pieces that cause havoc with the vacuum, and may cause problems if the pup swallows any. As for the hard rubber balls, they are supposed to be almost indestructible. It usually takes my German Shorthairs about a day and a half of steady work to gnaw them into oblivion. The longer you can prevent your pup from really gnawing on it instead of just teething – the longer it will last. However, once your pup gets focused on gnawing – the ball is doomed.

6

Some Thoughts About Training

There are two broad philosophies about hunting dog training in the United States. The first "breaking" school advocates doing minimal training of the dog until it is old enough to take the pressure of modern training methods. These experts advocate waiting until a dog is in the 10 month to 18 month window of age before beginning serious training and then "breaking" the dog with rather forceful training methods. This school of training has its roots in the professional trainers in the early part of the twentieth century that trained field trial dogs for wealthy patrons. Such trainers believed that early training of pups diminished their independence – a terrible sin for dogs that are judged in a large part on their independence and willingness to range far away from the handler.

I suspect that those trainers were probably right to an extent – but I also believe that their concerns are completely irrelevant to the hunter. Where the All Age field trialer wants a dog that is willing to run far away from the handler and work at distances of a quarter mile or more from the gun – these are not useful characteristics where the hunter is concerned. Encouraging this degree of independence in a pup is actually counterproductive for a hunter.

Professional trainers today also tend to belong to this school because this type of training, which tends to be concentrated in a relatively short period of time, is a more efficient way for them to conduct their business. To be fair, this predilection for "breaking" style training isn't merely an issue of financial self interest (though that element can't be denied). It is also because many trainers believe, with some justification, that they as professionals are more likely to give the dog the best possible training and avoid many of the pitfalls that amateur trainers often encounter. Most trainers working with adult dogs and forceful training methods can reliably "break" a dog and train it to be a dependable Pointer within eight weeks. Clients are willing to spend $500 or more per week as long as they know that the duration of training and their expenses will be limited to such a period of time.

This isn't to say that there aren't German Shorthairs whose independence, lack of natural instincts, and poor bidability make them better suited to "breaking." The field trial strains of German Shorthairs often require such handling. However, most traditional German Shorthairs can be easily trained by any owner without resort to hanging, dangling, shocking, choking, tripping, or some of the other forceful methods so often used in "breaking" dogs.

This can pose something of a problem for the German Shorthair owner because many, if not most, pointing dog training books are focused on 'breaking" dogs. Such books are often written by professionals who typically see more than their share of the "problem dogs." These are the dogs whose excessive independence, lack of bidability, difficulty in learning, poor mental attitude, or other problems, persuade their owners to send them to professional trainers. As such, the tendency of many of these books is to advocate forceful "breaking style" training that will overcome the resistance of all but the most obstinate dogs. However, I firmly believe such extremely forceful breaking methods are overkill for most well bred traditional German Shorthairs – and mistakes made using such methods often cause long term problems that require professional assistance to rectify.

The second "natural" school of training has its roots in the training traditionally done by hunters for centuries. It also draws upon modern knowledge of canine psychology, techniques and methods from the training of guide dogs for the blind, animal behaviorists, etc. This school starts training puppies at a very young age. Rather than using forceful methods to "break" an adolescent dog, this school focuses on teaching pups using canine psychology, instinct, and directed experience. At its heart this is the training school that is the most natural and comfortable for most people because it mimics the way we ourselves learn and the way we teach our children. It is the training school to which I belong –and which underlays the methods outlined in this book.

You don't have to be a tyrant to have a fine hunting dog.

At the heart of the natural school of training are a few core principals:

• Always use the least amount of force necessary to achieve the training objective. In this context, force is understood to entail physical coercion and/or the infliction of pain or distress – whether it is through beating, pinching, shocking, hanging, choking, or training methods that incorporate similar techniques.

The use of excessive force is an inefficient way to teach because it discourages the dog from problem solving for fear of "correction" and often causes unintended problems. It also tends to make these unintended problems more difficult to overcome because the pain and trauma inflicted often makes the dog afraid to do anything for fear of making a mistake.

Perhaps the classic example of this is what is called "bird blinking" – where a dog that has been forcefully punished around birds will associate the birds themselves with punishment and ignore or shy away from them in the field. The inappropriate use of excessive force can actually make a bird dog afraid of birds. Avoiding excessive force is one of the best ways to avoid causing such problems.

- Wherever possible, use the dog's natural instincts to help teach desired behaviors. As highly social animals each dog has a set of complex core social instincts that let it function as part of a larger social structure (pack). These same social instincts enable the dog to work as part of our social structure –and by understanding and using these instincts we can teach our dogs to be outstanding hunters without needing to force them into compliance. For example, by using our dog's natural instinct to chase, we can teach it the meaning of the Come command without having to yank it toward us with a rope (this will be described in the next chapter).
- Structure your training sessions to allow the dog to learn the lessons you want from its experiences. For example, if a dog learns that it can catch a bird without your help, then you are teaching it that it doesn't need you to hunt birds. If it learns that it can't catch a bird, and needs to point and wait for you to shoot the bird – then you are teaching it that in order for it to get a bird it needs to work with you as part of a team.
- Always behave as the pack leader. This doesn't mean that you have to fight for dominance with your dogs, or roll them over on their backs, or anything else to "establish" dominance. In fact, the alpha status is yours from the time you take your young pup home simply by the fact of your size and the dependence the pup has on you for food and shelter.

  The key isn't to establish yourself as an alpha – it's simply not to lose the alpha status you've already got. That alpha status is cemented by your consistently acting in a manner that ensures that you will always receive normal deference from your dog in the relationship you establish with it. I will discuss this aspect of training at greater length farther on because it is the area in which so many behavioral problems and dysfunctional canine/human relationships are rooted.
- Communicate clearly with your dog. This is easier said than done for a novice. Training and daily interaction helps develop this ability. On your part, you must learn to "read"

your dog – understanding what your dog is telling you and why. At the same time, your dog must learn to read you.

Typically, dogs do this far more easily than we do – to the point that they can read our body language and posture to receive a far more complex message than we are giving them verbally. Sometimes, these are actually contradictory messages – which can result in the dog receiving mixed messages. For example if we are angry about an extraneous matter our body language and tone may reflect that tenseness even as we try and portray a calm demeanor in our training. We have to learn to communicate with our dogs with our whole body in a manner that avoids giving contradictory messages. As we get more experienced in reading our dogs, this communication grows deeper and more profound – to the point that it can seem at times that hunter and dog can read each other's minds. Perhaps they can.

- Build a bond of trust and understanding with your dog. This will help lay a foundation for training, and make you a more effective hunting team. Members of a wolf pack in the wild have a highly intimate relationship with each other. They learn to understand each other's thought processes and to anticipate each other's reactions. They literally trust each other with their lives every time they hunt an animal larger and more powerful than they are. That trust and understanding is the basis for the cooperation that enables the wolf pack to bring down a moose or buffalo that weighs more than ten times the weight of an individual wolf.

To an extent, this is the same bond that we are building with our hunting dogs. One of the things that I like to point out to new hunters is that the most effective bird hunters and dog handlers use the least amount of commands in the field. They have achieved such a level of understanding and partnership with their dogs – and have become such a team – that verbal commands become almost unnecessary. Both of them know what they need to do, and what the other is going to do. A bond of this nature is built on love, trust and extensive interaction with each other. In my experience, a dog has to be a participating part of a family to be able to form this kind of bond – and dogs left outside in a kennel most of the time can't be expected to build the same kind of bond and relationship with the handler. As with most things in life, love and kindness pays off in all sorts of unexpected ways.

Having said all of this, perhaps a caveat is in order. This "natural" type of training tends to work best on well bred, cooperative dogs with strong natural pointing and retrieving instincts. Other "natural training" type programs such as those that train guide dogs for the blind, assistance dogs, and sniffer dogs go to great lengths to identify and select cooperative pups and discard those that don't meet their criteria. With German Shorthairs, the primary method we have to identify a pup with a cooperative nature and strong natural instincts is that it comes from parents and lines that have such characteristics. However, even from such lines, while unusual, it is possible to get problem pups with limited natural instincts, slow problem solving skills, and/or "lone wolf" tendencies.

Such an uncooperative dog with limited natural pointing and retrieving instincts may need the "boot camp" of breaking style training to be able to function at all as a hunting dog in the field. My own view is that the lack of such genetic characteristics in a hunting dog is such a handicap that if a dog hasn't shown some signs of responding to the natural training methods below by the age of 18 months – I personally would start over with a better bred dog. If you are not so inclined, nothing in the natural training regime should cause problems in sending your dog off to a professional trainer to be "broke." Fortunately, with well bred traditional German Shorthairs this will rarely be the case.

The traditional German Shorthair has a well deserved reputation for being easy to train. It is often recommended as a first dog for hunters because of its intelligence, it's strong willingness to please, it's strong natural pointing and retrieving instincts, and it's ability to learn quickly and to shrug off training mistakes. This makes German Shorthairs different from some other breeds. Most of the more forceful training methods in use today were developed to deal with highly independent field trial stock Pointers and English Setters.

Certainly, the vast majority of hunting German Shorthairs are successfully trained by their owners – and those who choose instead to use a professional miss out on a great deal of pleasant bonding time with their pup. While not "idiot proof" the traditional German Shorthair can generally be taught to be a fine hunting dog without using extremely forceful methods or expensive training equipment.

7

Building the Foundation

Experts say that most of the personality traits and characteristics that a person carries through their life are set during the time they are very young children. The same is true with dogs. Most of the personality characteristics and patterns of interaction that your dog will show as an adult hunting dog and family companion are set in these early days. The quality of your hunting dog in future years is primarily determined by how you treat it and what you teach it during these early months. What the puppy learns during these first six months to a large extent sets the foundation for the dog that it will become. I can't overstate the importance of getting this right. Fortunately, this is easy to do.

As with children, small puppies are literally learning sponges. From the time you bring the pup home, it will be learning. Your job, and it can sometimes be difficult, is to ensure that it learns how to be a good canine citizen, family member, and hunting partner. To do this requires some basic understanding of canine psychology, a clear idea of what you are trying to teach, and consistency in how you interact with your pup.

The first step in building the foundation is socialization. This is a fancy word for allowing the pup to have social experiences and build social bonds. This requires almost constant social interaction with you and the family, with other dogs and other people, travel to other places, etc. Socialization hones the pup's social skills, and lets it get comfortable with the larger world. A pup that learns to interact with other people and other dogs is less likely to become fearful of them and to bite.

Just as with human babies, such social interaction and the stimulation it brings also serves to open neural pathways in the pup's brain that enables it learn things faster and be more adaptive. Playing with your pup, letting it run afield, taking it to play with children and other dogs, are investments in the

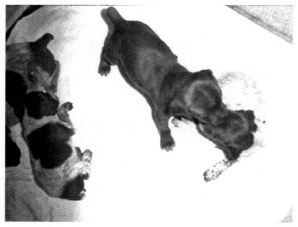
Puppies need to play and have a variety of experiences for their brains to develop fully.

quick wittedness of your dog that will make it easier to train and a better hunter. A pup that is kept in isolation in a kennel all day, and allowed only limited contact with humans or other dogs, is a pup that will likely be neurotic and have psychological problems down the road.

Over the years I've rescued such psychologically damaged German Shorthairs – and it is heartbreaking to realize that these problems could have been easily avoided simply by playing with the pup, and giving it love and attention.

As with small children, puppies need to learn from the earliest age that they are loved and that they can trust you to take care of them and keep them safe. Small puppies need plenty of holding, and stroking, and tactile reassurances. They also need to learn to identify your voice, and your scent in a positive setting. Holding a young pup close to your heart is a good way to do both – as is playing with the pup.

However, even at this age it is important that you be the senior partner. From the earliest times, we need to continue a relationship that makes canine deference, where the pup unquestioningly views you as the leader, the norm. This relationship that we have with the puppy needs to be a relationship that exists in dog terms as well as human – where the puppy instinctively understands what's going on and is comforted by the parameters. Too often humans get these things mixed up, and wind up sending mixed messages that encourage pups to challenge our directions.

This is why puppies should not be allowed on furniture on their own. We derive much of our authority in dog terms from our size and the fact that we tower over our canine companions. Taller tends to equal dominant in the dog world. As the pup gets older – a situation where the dog's eyes are physically on an equal level with the human's encourages the dog to think of itself of an equal instead of being lower in the pack hierarchy. This is another way that humans lose their authority and status. I will hold young puppies and dogs in my lap – but I don't often let them on the furniture next to me, nor do I let them sleep on my bed. While some would argue that a young pup is small enough that it won't view itself as an equal even if allowed to sit on the furniture, I would respond that you should start as you mean to continue. It is much harder to teach an adult dog not to do things it was permitted to do as a puppy than it is simply not to allow it to do those things in the first place. Too many problems down the road, including aggression problems (it isn't uncommon to come across dogs that will snap if their owners attempt to move them from the bed or furniture) can be traced back to such simple actions.

Another way that we reinforce our alpha status in canine terms is through our control of food. In canine society those lower in the pack hierarchy don't eat until those above them start –and the alphas control everyone's access to food. In a human household this is why questions of feeding the dog are so important. The act of feeding the dog reinforces that the human in control of the food is dominant over the dog receiving it. This is why dogs should NOT be left to self feed. The relationship between the human, food, and the dog needs to be obvious and clear to the dog. Actions such as giving the dog a biscuit in a manner that the human clearly controls are good ways to reinforce this in the dog's mind – while also making your dog happy. Dogs should be fed at regular times, and given a reasonable time to finish their food before it is put off limits. The dog should see the human both giving the food, and taking it away –and the human should be able to take the food away without growling or aggression from the pup. Such growling should be punished – it will become much more difficult to deal with if not dealt with at an early age. In mild cases the punishment can be as simple as making the dog sit and not returning the food until you get compliance (reinforcing status). All humans in the household should take turns in feeding the pup to reinforce their dominant status in the pack. That's a fancy way of saying that this will help avoid having a dominant dog try and bully household members as it ages.

This brings us to the topic of boundaries. While we want to build that bond of love and trust with our puppies, we will also need to set boundaries if we want a good canine citizen that we can turn into a quality gun dog. Puppies need to learn that there are things that are acceptable and things that are unacceptable. This process starts from the minute you bring your pup home. We started early with our pup with our housebreaking training to teach them that there are places to relieve themselves and places where they can't. There are other boundaries we need to set. And as with small children, puppies will keep on testing these boundaries to see if they can make them change. If they find that they can, then they have learned that they are the ones who determine where the boundaries are set. I noted earlier that owners tend to lose the alpha status they get automatically when they get a small pup – and having unclear boundaries is one of the earliest and easiest ways they start to do so.

We set boundaries based upon two main factors – what human society requires of a dog in terms of manners and canine citizenship, and what dog society requires in terms of maintaining a proper relationship between the leader and pack member. Often the two overlap.

In terms of setting boundaries from a human standpoint we want to teach the puppy to respond to its name, to get it habituated to collar and leash, to housebreak the pup, teach it not to jump up or beg, and instill in it a habit of deference and obedience.

PUPPIES AND DISCIPLINE

Perhaps the most important command in teaching boundaries is the command NO! This command comes naturally from humans, it is what we typically say when we catch a pup doing something wrong. To a large extent it is

Puppies are easily harmed when they are small, so discipline needs to mild

understood naturally by small pups because of the volume, tone of voice, and body language that invariably accompanies the command. However, when a simple No is not enough to get through to a recalcitrant pup it is important to remember that any physical coercion following the command needs to be mild.

Pups are easily harmed when they are small – and things such as spankings with a newspaper or other object are inappropriate and unnecessary. It is all right to give a pup a mild swat on the rear with the fingers of your hand if it is refusing to pay attention to you and ignoring your directions. However, before you do so you should always ask whether the swat will teach the pup anything other than to be afraid of you? If you are swatting a puppy because it relieved itself on the floor a half hour before – all you are doing is taking out your anger on your puppy, and teaching it to be wary of you. The puppy won't associate the punishment with the action – all it will see is a random act of violence.

Most often the only thing needed to discipline a young pup is tone of voice, followed by gentle physical restraint if necessary. A puppy that is sniffing at things it shouldn't, or looking to chew on something it shouldn't, can be told a stern No, and then picked up and relocated if reinforcing the No is necessary. A pup sniffing as though it needs to relieve itself can be picked up and taken outside.

Squirt bottles:

A common squirt bottle filled with water is also a fine tool with which to discipline puppies and even larger dogs. Pups engaging in unacceptable behavior such as barking, chewing, or inappropriate play can be admonished with a couple of squirts in the face. Obviously, you don't want to do this from a range close enough to cause harm. However, at normal ranges this can be a remarkably effective way of getting a pup or dog to stop doing something they shouldn't be doing. Oddly enough, even dogs that love swimming and the water, will react negatively to the squirt bottle.

Snappers:

These are used to help keep puppies and dogs off of the furniture or counters. While this is fairly easy to do when you are around the house, during the daytime when folks are working or running errands enforcement can be difficult. Most German Shorthairs learn that they can sneak onto the furniture when nobody is around – and because it is forbidden fruit they often do. Not only does this blur the boundary lines – it can also result to damage to the furniture from muddy paws and nails used to dig and make cushions more comfortable.

There are electronic pads that are made to keep dogs off of furniture – some deliver a mild shock, others sound an alarm. These can both work fine – but they are a bit expensive. A cheaper alternative is what I call snappers. These are old fashioned, spring powered, wire mouse (not rat) traps to which a small piece of cardboard has been taped. This cardboard is taped to the spring loaded arm that is designed to swing down and kill the mouse when triggered. The purpose of the cardboard is to eliminate any remote possibility of the trap causing damage to toes, lips, or ears when the arm comes down. Once the mousetraps are made safe with the cardboard I arm them and put them on furniture, counters, and other places where errant Shorthairs shouldn't be, but have ventured. When triggered, the mousetraps will make a loud snap, amplified by the cardboard, and may even get in a pinch or two. This should be enough to make the dog quickly back down – and avoid a repeat experience.

Repellants:

Pups can also be passively restrained from mischief through the use of substances that repel the pup. There are sprays such as Bitter Apple that can be applied to electrical cords, furniture, etc. to keep the pup from chewing on them. Some work well, and some not so well. One of the best of these substances in my experiences is Tabasco sauce, or a similar hot sauce. It has a very distinctive smell – and once the pup learns to associate the burn of Tabasco with its smell, anything that smells like Tabasco will be safe. Cayenne pepper is another useful substance that is particularly good for sprinkling over garbage to thwart those dogs who like to go prospecting in the trash (almost all German Shorthairs).

Physical restraint:

If a pup requires stern measures to get its attention – I next resort to picking the pup up by the scruff of its neck. I do this by pinching the skin at the scruff of the neck, and lifting the pup off of its feet. In more serious situations I may also growl at it. This is one way a mother uses to express displeasure with what a pup is doing – so the pup is instinctively programmed to understand this action. It is also a clear expression of dominance. When picked up, the pup will stick all four legs out in a braced position and cease struggling. Once you get this reaction you can put the pup down – it should have gotten the message. If the pup still hasn't gotten the message, you can repeat the action. One should never shake a puppy or handle it roughly when holding it by the scruff – this is not only unnecessary it can cause serious harm to a young pup. Picking a pup up by the scruff of the neck should only be done to small puppies. By the time they reach ten to twelve weeks or so they get too big.

Obedience lays the foundation for performance in the field.

Time out:

Another important tool in enforcing discipline is the time out. While this becomes a more important tool with adolescent dogs it is also useful for puppies. Essentially this entails removing the pup from the social interaction of the pack for a short period of time. Whether it is confining the pup to a crate, a kennel, or the back yard – the point is to keep it separate from the fun for a short period. In the context of discipline, you want to impose the time out as close as possible to the bad behavior you are seeking to punish. As a social animal – being separated from others is a significant punishment for any dog. Obviously, you don't want to do this to excess or you risk isolating the pup and creating psychological problems. However, it can be an extremely useful way of reinforcing dominance and punishing the pup without inflicting pain.

BASIC OBEDIENCE

We teach the basic obedience commands to enable us to exert a degree of control over the actions of our canine companions – and to give them the manners that make them good canine citizens. These same commands serve a similar function both in the hunting field and in the home. By teaching these commands to our young pups, when they are actively learning and easier to teach, we are instilling knowledge that will pay dividends over the rest of the dog's life. We are also building a habit of obedience – one habit that we want our dogs to have throughout their life. Fortunately, these commands are

Sit is one of the most useful commands for both home and field.

simple and easy to teach to young pups

Sit/Stay

The purpose of the sit command is to stop the dog and get it to remain in one place; the stay command keeps them there until the handler releases them. As with most obedience commands, we want to combine the verbal command with an equivalent hand command. This will give you the ability to exert some control over the dog when it can't hear you because of excessive distance, background noise, or interference by cover. Because sitting is natural to dogs – it is a normal observation position for dogs trying to keep an eye on things or to puzzle something out – it is an easy command to teach. In fact it is so easy that almost every dog will learn to do so whether formally taught or not. Dogs will typically sit in response to certain stimuli, so all we need to do is to trigger the action and then connect the command to the action in the dog's mind.

Sit/Stay is one of the most commonly used commands around the house and is often used in the field (particularly while duck or dove hunting). It has obvious safety benefits, such as being able to stop a dog before they enter a danger zone such as a busy road, or to keep them still in a duck blind and out of the line of fire. It also is a command that reinforces the leader/pack member relationship – so it is a good command to reestablish control over a rambunctious pup or dog. By having a reliable "stop" command such as sit/stay, hunters can gain a moment to calm down an overexcited dog, or to redirect a dog's focus.

In Europe, sit is one of the commands routinely taught to dogs that are expected to hunt waterfowl and big game as well as upland birds. This command has been taught as a matter of course to hunting dogs for centuries. It is also an almost essential manners command for an indoor dog. However, in the US there is a school of trainers who have come to claim that teaching sit will encourage a dog to sit on point. This is not true – as demonstrated by the European experience – and should be treated as one of the old wives tales without foundation in fact. Pointing dogs that sit on point do so because of excessive training pressure, confusion, boredom, and/or a lack of focus and intensity. German Shorthairs should be taught as a matter of course to sit because of their versatile hunting roles – and in nearly forty years of training and owning German Shorthairs I have never seen any problems engendered by doing so.

To teach a young pup to sit, quite often all it takes is giving the command while standing erect and pointing up with the index finger. Young dogs that don't automatically react to this, can have their rear ends pushed gently down into a sitting position (a slight pinch on top of the butt while pushing down often helps make things easier) while you firmly say the command sit, and give the hand command. They will soon understand what is desired – and make the connection between the command and the action.

Once a dog has been taught sit, teaching stay is simply a matter of having the dog sit, issuing the stay command with a hand signal with the palm flat and facing the dog, and walking slowly away. When the dog moves to follow tell the dog "no," move in and put it back sitting *in the exact same place it moved from*. Repeat this exercise until the dog will sit still reliably until you move some distance away -and then release the dog with an upbeat "OK" command. The dog will soon understand what both commands mean.

If you desire you can expand on the stay command by moving out of direct sight of the dog, but where you can keep the dog under observation. Moving behind a bush or around a corner where the dog can't see you will typically get the dog to follow to attempt to locate you. Once again, you need to stop the dog as soon as possible after it moves, and return it to the exact space it moved from. Repetition will teach the dog to stay reliably until released.

Down

Teaching the pup to lie down is a simple extension of the sit/stay command. Essentially we are using the same teaching method for a different physical position. Down is a very important command for dogs living inside because it is the command that tells the pup to cease activity and go into "rest" mode. If you are going to use the verbal command "down" be sure not to use the same command to attempt to stop the dog from jumping up, or for getting off the furniture. By trying to use one command for three different actions – you will only create confusion. I mentioned earlier that it was important to have clear communication with your dog – and down is a classic case of a command that is often muddled.

To teach the pup down, first have the pup sit. Praise the pup once it sits. Then point your index finger down at the place you want the pup to lay (initially where the pup is sitting), and push the pup gently down to a laying position. Don't push too forcefully or you will turn the exercise into a test of wills that we want to avoid. If the pup resists too much, you can gently sweep out its front legs to get the pup's belly on the ground. Once you have the pup laying with its belly down – take some

A dog that doesn't lay down on command isn't fully trained. Flick, a New Zealand German Shorthair owned by Margaret Cotton shows how it's done.

time to pet and praise it. The objective of the training is to get the pup to associate the action of laying down with the verbal and hand command – and to understand that compliance brings positive reinforcement. Once the pup understands what is wanted, then you only have to deal with compliance.

Once you have the pup obeying the "down" command reliably, you can further expand the down command to the point where you can get the dog to lay down in a specific place by pointing at the place you want the pup to lay. Start by having the pup sit and lie down right in front of you, with your finger pointing where the pup will lay. Move again and call the pup to you, have it sit, and then give the command down pointing clearly to a place to one side of the pup. When the pup goes to lie down at a place you didn't point at, pick it gently up and move it to the place you indicated with your finger –and then move back to your original point. This will at first be confusing to the pup, but through repetition the pup will soon learn to recognize that the finger will be pointing to where you want the pup to execute the command. It is important during this process that you have patience and keep your temper because ill advised punishment or shouting can persuade the dog not to lie down or sit at all for fear of angering you.

Again, we build the habit of compliance by repetition – not the infliction of pain or distress. However, repetition doesn't mean that we force the pup to sit and lay down for hours at a time, until it is bored stiff. Young pups have short attention spans, so extended drills are counterproductive. Giving the commands a few times per day – or doing training sessions perhaps ten or fifteen minutes at a session – will be more than enough to teach the commands to a young pup. The most important part is that when you give the sit and down commands, they must end with the pup complying with the command and getting praise and love.

The "Come" command.

If I had to pick one single command that every German Shorthair should know and reliably obey, it would be the "come" command. This is the command that tells the dog to immediately stop whatever they are doing and return to the handler. From a safety standpoint, this is the most important command a dog can learn. It allows a handler to call a dog away from potential or imminent dangers such as a busy road, an angry rattlesnake, or the local rancher's prize bull.

From the hunter's perspective it is a vital command for a pup to learn because it is a foundation command for teaching a dog to reliably retrieve game. It also allows a hunter to monitor and care for their dog over the course of a hunt, giving thirsty dogs water, pulling cactus spines, checking for cuts and abrasions, etc. In terms of manners, it also allows a handler to call their dog back from areas in which other hunters are already working, or to bring in a misbehaving dog.

Teaching a young pup to come is relatively easy because it is a natural instinct for young pups to want to be close to the members of the pack. When you start teaching this command to the pup, you want to do so in an enclosed area such as a fenced yard or even a living room to enable you to keep some

A dog must come reliably when commanded - even when hot and tired.

control over the proceedings. This place should be relatively free of distractions such as other dogs, playing children, etc.

Most puppies can be taught to come at an early age simply by bending down and calling their name. In the way dogs interpret body language, bending down or lowering yourself close to their level is signaling equality and welcome. The closer to their level you get, the stronger this signal you send. It indicates that you don't have aggressive intent and want social contact. Basically this reassures the pup that they will receive a warm welcome if they do come bounding over –as they almost invariably do.

The biggest problem in teaching come this way to young dogs is their short attention span. They get easily distracted by smells, butterflies, sparrows, etc. and it can sometimes be difficult to get their attention without shouting at a level that frightens them. Some experts advise giving the command only once, and then going to physically get the pup (this is where the enclosed space helps). I tend to do things a little differently. With a pup, I will usually give the command once, and then if there is no response, I will give the command again accompanied by clapping hands to get their attention. If that doesn't get a response, I will give the command, rise and move *away* from the pup clapping my hands. The pup's natural instinct to chase should kick in and it should come bounding over to see what's going on. I then turn and welcome the pup's compliance. In any of these cases, when a pup does come in, it should be praised and petted - teaching it that this is the desired response to the command.

It's useful to reiterate this point – if a pup is dawdling or not coming quickly to you, move *away* from the pup. Our normal instinct is to move closer to the pup to "force" compliance as well as making it easier for the pup to comply. This is exactly the wrong response from a dog perspective. If we are conforming our movements to the pup's actions – then the pup is training us rather than vice versa. The vast majority of the time the pup must conform its movements to your directions or it is not obeying. Once again, letting the pup control who is moving toward whom is a simple, subtle way in which dog owners lose pack status and inadvertently encourage a dog not to give them the deference they are due.

With older, or more independent, dogs that won't respond to these methods, the standard method of teaching come is with a long lead. Usually the dog is told to sit/stay, the handler walks out to the end of the lead, and then giving the come command, pulls the dog toward them. Again, a dog that responds willingly should be praised. The object is the same as above, to teach the dog the desired response to the come command. Once they understand this, then your focus needs to change to enforcement of compliance rather than teaching. I prefer not to use this technique for teaching come if I can avoid it because it often creates an adversarial situation between the dog and trainer that I feel interferes with learning. I prefer creating teaching situations, wherever possible, where I get willing compliance from an enthusiastic dog rather than forced compliance from an uncomfortable dog. However, there are dogs that sometimes give you little choice.

Two words of caution about teaching the come command. The first is never discipline a dog, either verbally or physically, when it is coming in response to your come command - no matter how tardy the response or how angry you are. Doing so teaches the dog that responding to come results in punishment, and is the best way to ensure a dog that won't respond reliably to come. The second is to not let a dog get away with willful disobedience of the command once they know it. If a dog ignores a come command, and you are sure it's willful (and not, for example, because it is locked up on point or couldn't hear you), then your priority at that point should be to enforce compliance. For a young dog, one of the most effective ways of doing this is to sit down behind a piece of cover and hide. Once you hide you need to be completely quiet. After anywhere from five minutes to a half hour the pup will get alarmed by your disappearance and come to try and find you. Often it will circle around behind you and follow your trail to you. At times you will hear its barks and whines as panic sets in. Use your judgment about when to stand up and let the pup see you, or when to holler for it. Your pup should be overjoyed and very relieved to find you – and you should welcome it's return with some petting and kind words. I'll often wag a finger at the pup, and give it a mild verbal reprimand for not responding to come – but don't impose any physical punishment at all. Once you've re-established contact and moved out again, wait a minute or two and then call the dog to come again. You want to reestablish that habit of compliance – and if the pup comes then you have done that.

Always remember, it is NOT all right to punish a dog for not coming if it hasn't yet really learned what the come command means.

Kennel or Crate command

This is another command that is easy to teach to a young pup that will pay dividends down the line. As we noted, in the course of housebreaking the pup, the pup will be sleeping in its crate. We want to make this a positive experience so that the pup enjoys going into its "den." The easiest way to teach this command is to place a dog biscuit or small piece of cheese in the kennel when you first start placing the pup in the kennel. Put the pup in front of the kennel and give the command. The pup will soon learn to associate the place and the command – and to understand that the command means to go inside the kennel. If the pup shies at the entrance, tell it NO, physically restrain it and point it back into the kennel while giving the "Kennel" command again. As with other commands, once the pup complies it should be praised and petted.

A crate should be a place of comfort for a dog, whether resting within, or even snoozing on top.

The reason this command will be important down the line is that it is much safer and more convenient to transport a dog in its crate. For most of us who hunt and don't live someplace where we can start hunting out the back door, transporting our dogs is part of life. In those cases when our dogs have rolled in the remains of something long dead, or had an unfortunate tussle with a skunk – being able to keep them confined in a washable crate rather than the car upholstery is a true bonus. This is why having a dog that is comfortable in its crate, and willing to enter the crate on command, makes life much easier. As with other commands, it is much easier to teach this command to a puppy than it is with a rambunctious adolescent.

The Release Command – OK

As we teach the pup to obey commands such as those outlined above, we also need to teach it a command telling it when it is all right to stop complying with the command. A well trained pup should know not only when it has to stop and

123

obey, but also when it is free to continue its own activities. Obviously, if we have the pup sitting and staying, or laying down, we don't want it to stay that way for the rest of its life. We need a command that will let the pup know that we have moved on and that further compliance with the previous command is no longer necessary. Essentially, this is the equivalent of the military "dismissed" command.

The easiest release command, and the one I use, is a simple "OK." In earlier times, trainers often gave the command "hie on." To teach this command, we simply use it as the final half of our sit/stay command, and our down command. When we teach the pup to sit, and it has complied and been praised for compliance – we release it with the release command OK. This should be given in an enthusiastic tone of voice and accompanied by a physical action that lets the pup knows that we are done with the lesson – such as reaching down and petting up the pup. Puppies usually learn to understand the release command quite readily as long as it is used consistently. This means that pups that move onward from a command without being given the release command should be forced back into compliance. So if a pup decides to get up from the sit position without being given the "OK" – it needs to be put back into the sitting position, at the original place from which it moved, and given the sit command again. After it has sat for a while you can give it the release command. The pup needs to learn that it has to obey until you release it.

CONCLUSION

These basic obedience commands are ones that a young pup will typically learn quite quickly. Often it may only take a few minutes for a smart pup to learn each of these commands, and with repetition and plenty of praise and positive reinforcement the pup should get quite adept at these commands within a week or two. Getting the pup to obey these commands reliably and enthusiastically at a young age will pay big dividends as the dog gets older.

8

Building the Gun Dog to Be

Michelangelo, when asked how he could sculpt such beautiful masterpieces out of blocks of stone, reportedly said that the statue was already in the marble, his job was merely to chip away the stone surrounding it. To a large extent, that's the same with a young German Shorthair. The hunting dog is already in the pup – our job is simply to bring it out.

If you have chosen a well bred traditional German Shorthair pup, much of what you want the pup to do will be in its genes. Things like pointing game birds, retrieving, swimming, backing, working cover, and taking field direction are part of the pup's DNA. It is our job to bring those instincts to the fore in a manner that fosters teamwork and makes the pup into a competent hunting dog.

One of the advantages that we as hunters have over professional trainers is time. Professional trainers are almost always "on the clock." Few hunters can afford to spend more than two or three thousand dollars to have their pup trained – and with the costs of food, accommodation, birds and training equipment most pros can't turn a profit charging less than a few hundred dollars per week. This means that from a financial standpoint, a Pro typically has to produce a trained bird dog in six to eight weeks. This requires intense training, which in turn requires dogs with the maturity to handle such training. This is why you are unlikely to get from a pro a trained gun dog that is younger than a year of age.

As hunters who live with our dogs, we therefore have ten months of extra time to train our pups to be a competent gun dog at the same age as if we had waited and sent it off to be trained... Bluntly put, we have the luxury of time. We don't have to put a great deal of pressure on our pup – or adhere to any strict timeline. In fact, the pressure that most amateurs put on their German Shorthairs doesn't come from the requirements of the training methods, it comes from the ego and expectations of the owner/trainer.

Such influences are almost always negative. A good friend of mine, Web Parton, who is one of the top professional dog trainers in the country, once told me that the vast majority of his business was correcting the problems caused by owners who tried to train their own dogs. As noted in earlier sections, the number one cause of such problems is owners who use too much force and put too much stress on their dogs – with unintended consequences.

This is a long winded way of saying that you need to put your ego and your expectations aside when you start training your German Shorthair. Each pup is an individual that matures at its own rate, and has its own mix of genetic characteristics. As a consequence, each learns at its own pace. This is why rushing can often do more harm than good when it comes to training hunting dogs.

Richard Wolters one of the early modern advocates of the "natural school" of dog training and the author Gun Dog, one of the great hunting dog training books, included a timeline for training in his book. While I'm convinced he intended the timeline to serve as a general guideline – over the years many have interpreted the timeline as being written in stone and have had problems trying to meet it. Of the criticism that has been leveled at the book over the years, the criticism that he didn't make it clear enough that the timeline was flexible, is the one with which I have some sympathy. So for future reference, the timelines I quote in this book are general in nature –and flexible. If your pup takes longer to get to a certain point than another fellow's Shorthair does – don't give it any concern.

In my experience the vast majority of hunting dogs aren't legitimately reliable hunting dogs until the end of their second season. Puppies that are near perfect at 8 months often have a sophomore slump at 18 months. Puppies that seem to have learned nothing but mischief by 10 months sometimes come on like gangbusters in their second season. Some breeds, such as English Setters, can take even longer to mature and may not get their stride until their third year.

Using these training methods, and most others, if you have a pup with the genes you will have a competent hunting partner by the time the dog is two years of age. Until that time,

126

With good genes, patience, teaching skills, and plenty of field time you can turn your pup into a skilled hunter.

the pup's progress will depend on a variety of variables, from your teaching and canine communication skills, to field time, to the easy availability of wild birds, to the pup's personality and genetic inheritance.

As a general outline I like to tell hunters that using this training regime a puppy will be more help than hindrance in the field by the time it is six months to a year old. By more help than hindrance I mean that the pup will point, and retrieve birds and waterfowl, but it will likely still have problems handling game with polish. German Shorthairs this age will still make puppy mistakes such as accidentally bumping birds – no matter how talented they are. This is a good thing – because your pup will learn from each and every mistake if you allow them, and become a progressively better hunting dog.

To help them learn and grow, first and foremost you need to have patience and keep your temper under control. Guaranteed, the first time you try and show off your little genius to a hunting buddy – the pup that never made a mistake will spend the day pulling every bonehead dog move ever invented. Not only will it forget all of its training, it will invent new ways to ruin your hunting and embarrass you. If you can't shrug that off, laugh, and chalk it up to experience – you aren't going to do a good job training your pup. And if your buddy can't, then you should probably look for a better hunting buddy.

If I had to identify the number one reason that promising pups fail to become good gun dogs – I would unhesitatingly say that the inability of their owners to control their temper would be it. By a long shot. A hot tempered trainer that is constantly punishing a dog is a tragedy. Dogs that manage to become gun dogs after being trained by such a person do so despite the trainer, not because.

The second reason would be the impatience and frustration of the owner – demanding that the dog learn on their artificial schedule rather than the dog's natural schedule. Where this most often surfaces is in a competitive fellow with a young pup who insists that his pup outperform all other pups of the same age. If this fellow hears that another has a pup that is pointing perfectly at six months, he'll push his pup to do so at five months. If he hears that a pup is swimming and retrieving waterfowl at seven months, he'll push his pup to do so at six months. In the process, he will almost always do harm to the pup. Again, those pups that become good gun dogs after being trained by a trainer who's "trying to keep up with the joneses" do so despite their trainer, not because of them.

STARTING OUT

To a German Shorthair puppy the most fun you can have is being in the field with your master exploring and learning to hunt. The pup is instinctively programmed to seek out and point birds, to swim, and to retrieve objects. Getting the chance to experience those things is a true treat –for even very young pups. This is what makes training puppies so easy –and so much fun.

The essence of training a young pup is to structure "play" so that the pup begins to learn how to do the things their instincts are urging them to do anyway. In fact, as the Michelangelo quote implies above, in many cases we will simply be encouraging the development of actions that the pup is starting to exhibit on its own –and channeling them into proper hunting behaviors.

A classic example of this is picking up and carrying. It is quite common for German Shorthair pups to start picking up and carrying objects from a very early age. This typically evolves into the pup picking up and carrying objects to you – either to show you the object, or to encourage you to play with them with the object. This instinctive action is the foundation for retrieving.

Young German Shorthairs often start to show their pointing instincts at an early age as well. Puppies may "point" objects of curiosity and fascination such as butterflies, grasshoppers, sparrows, etc. Puppies may also pause before they pounce on their toys. That pause before the pounce is the instinctive foundation for the point.

Playing "Fetch" – teaching the retrieve

I like to start young pups off playing fetch almost as soon as they come home with me. Most puppies are programmed instinctively to chase and grab small moving objects – although they may not have the muscular coordination yet to do so with polish. Remember, all training done with puppies eight to twelve weeks of age needs to be done on a non-slip surface to avoid injury. Puppies this young lack muscular development, and can easily injure a leg or joint slipping on slippery surface.

Fetch training is easiest started out in the house. The best place to start such training is in a carpeted hallway. The hallway will effectively limit the pup's movements so that they have little choice but to bring back the object that they chased down the hall –and the carpeting makes a firm footing for puppy limbs.

As for the object to be "fetched" it needs to be of a size and weight that a puppy can easily pick up, and it needs to be easily thrown inside the house. A rolled up sock is the best object I've found to use for young pups. Roll it up as firmly as you can, and tuck it inside the opening of the sock to make a firm "ball." Take the pup to the entrance to the hallway and toss the sock down the hallway while saying "fetch." Give the command in a firm tone of voice, but don't shout. You want a command the pup will hear, but in a tone and noise level that won't scare it. Make sure the pup spots the sock as you throw it, and sees it moving down the hallway. This should trigger the instinct to chase and capture.

When the pup picks up the sock bend down and call the pup to you (clapping your hands helps). (This drill will help reinforce the come command that you are teaching as well.) When the pup comes to you, praise it heavily. You want the pup to understand that bringing the sock back to you is good. Then, reach your hand out, palm up and grab the sock in the pup's mouth. Firmly say the command "Give" while gently pressing the pup's lips against its teeth. This should persuade the pup to open its mouth, and you can remove the sock. If the pup struggles to hold on to the sock, blowing a gentle puff of air into its nose will persuade it drop the sock quickly. Stand up and throw the sock again – repeating the drills as above. It's important that you do this as soon as you remove the sock from the pup's mouth, because you want the pup to learn that if it brings back the sock it will be rewarded with another throw. Just as we will eventually want the dog to recognize that the reward for retrieving a bird is the ability to go out and find more birds.

If the pup doesn't come back –but decides to ignore the come command and chew on the sock or attempt to run off with it – you need to catch the pup and, saying the "give" command, remove the sock from its mouth. Go back to the entrance to the hallway – encouraging the pup to follow by enticing it with the sock. Repeat the drill. Again, what we are trying to teach the pup is that it has to bring the sock back to you in order to get to continue playing.

If the pup becomes rambunctious during this training and decides that it would rather attempt to run off and play by itself with the sock instead of bringing it back to you – stop the play and put the sock up.

As the pup gets a bit older and more reliable at obeying the command, the game can be moved into the yard. We don't want to move it outside, or to other rooms in the house, until the pup has the basic sequence down – throw, chase and grab, bring back, give –because we want to keep it easy to intervene and correct the pup. In a hallway this is easy, in a yard it is difficult. Once the pup is reliably fetching, this won't be an issue – but we don't want to create a situation where the pup can turn the training on its head and get us to chase it for any distance.

With the simple game of throwing the sock for the pup we are teaching the pup to mark, find and retrieve objects when we give the "Fetch" command, and to release them into our hand when we command "give." As the pup gets older we can graduate to using a tennis ball, a canvas retrieving dummy, and then birds.

Bringing out the Pup's Point

As mentioned before, pointing is, or should be, a natural instinct that all traditional German Shorthairs possess. Essentially, it is an exaggerated pause in the hunting stalk before a pounce that has been extended by selective breeding for centuries.

In the past, hunters normally brought out a pup's natural pointing instinct by exposing a young dog to healthy populations of wild birds. While not advisable for very young pups (who can be scratched or harmed by birds almost as big, or bigger, than they are), this is still one of the best ways to train a young pointing dog. Wild birds are the best teachers for a pointing dog – indeed a pointing dog can't reach its full potential without the finishing that wild birds offer. However, where our great grandfathers may have had the luxury of healthy populations of wild birds living in the back forty, or just down the lane – most of us are no longer so fortunate. We have to improvise.

The best tool I've found for bringing out the point of a young pup is the "wing on a string." This consists of a long pole, a length of clear monofilament fishing line, and the dried wing of a game bird. For the pole, I use an old fly rod of about 9 ½ feet – but a cane rod or other rod of a similar length will work just as well. To the tip of the rod I tie a length of monofilament line about 8 feet long. To the other end of the line I tie the wing of a game bird. I prefer to use the wings of wild birds that I hunt, so the most common wing I use is a Gambel's quail wing. If you are primarily a grouse hunter, you should use a grouse wing if you can; if you hunt pheasants a pheasant wing, etc.

The reason that we want to use the wing of the wild bird that we hunt is that we want the pup to associate the smell of the bird with pointing. The best way to preserve such wings for use with puppies is to clip them off at the joint, and then put them into a paper bag and cover them with salt. Leave them in a dry place to cure. The salt will dry and disinfect them, without being harmful to the pup. However, if you don't have any dried wings of your own, you can order some wings from hunting dog suppliers such as Cabela's, or from fly fishing shops that carry fly tying materials. If you aren't sure that such wings were preserved with chemicals safe for the pup – wash them in warm soapy water and rinse them off, then allow them to dry in the open air before allowing the pup to mouth the wing

While the wing on the string can be easily used in the back yard, or even in the house if you have an understanding spouse – it is best used in an area where clipped grass gives way to unmown grass or weeds about four to six inches high. The reason for this is that once we have to the pup interested in the wing and pointing, we are going to want to cast the wing into short cover that the pup can easily negotiate, but which will hide the wing from sight and force it to locate the wing using its nose.

To get the pup interested in the wing, it is rarely necessary to do more than to dangle it or drag it in front of the pup. The smell of the wing should be intensely attractive to the pup, which will typically chase and try and catch the wing. This is good. We want the pup to be enthusiastic about chasing and catching the wing –even though we won't let them catch it without permission.

However, we also want to remember that the wing is a substitute for a bird, and it has to behave like the birds that the pup will later encounter. What the wing on the string does is lay the foundation for an easy transition to wild birds – but it only does that if the wing behaves like a bird. So once we have the puppy chasing the wing we need to "flush" it into the air by jerking it upwards with the rod and casting it away from the pup but within its eyesight. Every time the pup gets within a safety range around the wing, say about a foot or eighteen inches, you need to flush it into the air where the pup can't catch it. At first this will result in the pup madly dashing about trying to catch the wing before it takes flight. Depending upon the pup's problem solving abilities, it will soon begin to puzzle out other ways of catching the wing. This takes longer with some pups than others, but most reach this point relatively quickly.

At this point the pup will charge toward the wing, but slow down as it gets close to the wing – anticipating the flush. Again, we need to keep that safety zone around the wing in our mind and trigger the flush once the pup breaks that barrier – regardless of how slow the pup is creeping. As we noted above, the point is a pause in the stalk, so once we have a pup slowing down and stalking the wing – we are halfway there.

As the wing continues to flush as the pup gets too close, the pup will soon resort to pointing – pausing at the edge of the safety zone, fully focused on the wing, trying to figure out a good time to pounce. When the pup first points, even if it is just for a second or two, you want to praise the pup lavishly – until it moves. You can provide negative feedback to the pup once it starts to move by uttering something like uh-uh, or tsk-tsk. We don't want to use a NO! because at this stage we don't want to do anything that might give the impression that it shouldn't be trying to seek and point the wing. We are letting the pup know that pointing is what it should be doing as a hunting dog, and that we want it to do so. Again, we want to give positive reinforcement for desired behaviors –and not do anything that might frighten the pup or make it shy of finding the "bird."

As we continue to flush the wing once the pup has started pointing what we will find is that the points will typically last longer and longer. At first the pup is likely to simply halt, gather itself, and then rush in. As the wing continues to flush, the pup will start waiting longer and longer to see if it can lull the wing into a false sense of security, then it will pounce.

Again, we need to quietly praise the pup as it points, without distracting its attention from the wing.

A pup can soon get tired of constantly chasing anything without catching it, so it is necessary to occasionally let the pup "catch" the wing to keep it interested. However, this needs to be structured in such a way so that the pup doesn't come to believe that it can catch the wing on its own. To do this, once the pup is pointing staunchly, I give the release command OK which should trigger it to rush in and pounce. I let the pup grab the wing and mouth it for a while, perhaps prancing around proudly with its prize, before having it "Give" and going back to the game.

Once the pup has the hang of the game on mown grass or dirt, we need to move the training to rougher ground, where the wing can be hidden from view. Tufts of grass four to six inches high are perfect cover – though any cover that will hide the wing from the pups view will do. The reason that we want to be able to hide the wing from view is because birds are rarely found out in the open. We want our pup to be learning to use its nose to locate and identify the wing, and to identify how close it can get before the wing flushed wild.

As the pup gets more sophisticated at the game it is going to become necessary to try and keep it from seeing where the wing "lands." To do this, I cast the wing rapidly back and forth in the air – causing the pup to turn and twist to try and keep track – and I cast the wing into the area towards which the pup's back is turned. I then encourage the pup to "find the bird," and it will take off on a search. If the pup gets within the safety zone of the wing while rushing about searching, I flush the wing. We want to teach the pup to use its nose and to search – not simply to chase. As we continue this drill, the pup should learn to settle down and search at a pace that will allow it to scent the wing and point without causing it to flush.

Once the pup is finding and pointing the hidden wing reliably, holding point until released, and showing the kind of polish on the wing that we want them to show in the field, we have succeeded in laying the foundation. In my experience, with traditional German Shorthairs, the transition to wild birds in the field is typically fairly easy once a pup has such a foundation with the wing on a string.

Once the pup has been introduced to wild birds in the field and is pointing them staunchly, the wing on a string can be put up. Its function is to teach the basics of pointing and lay a foundation for introduction to wild birds. Once that introduction has been successfully accomplished – the need for the wing disappears.

Introduction to the field

The field to a German Shorthair is a magical, liberating place, as it is for all of us who hunt. It is a place where we can shrug off the trappings of civilization and rejoin the hunting pack. It is a place where the bindings and limitations of everyday life slip away – and life gains new focus.

This transformation can be intoxicating for a young pup – inciting it to run riot and forget about the pack. In a wolf pack, the members can run down a recalcitrant youngster and bring it to its senses. We have a window of time when the pup is still young and hasn't fully developed, where we have the same ability, but that window of time is fairly short. By the time a pup is six months old, it can typically outrun its owner. The only control we have over the pup at that age is its natural social/pack instincts, the bond we have built with it, the habit of deference that we have instilled, and the response to the obedience commands we have taught.

We also need to remember that the field can be a dangerous place for a young pup. The pup that in a few months will become a formidable predator, at eight weeks of age is potentially a nice meal for many predators. In the natural world, pups at this age would be closely guarded by their parents and the other pack members – and we have the same obligation to protect our young charges.

I remember one spring, just after the dawn of the new millennium, when I had taken Greta, one of my young pups along with three of my older German Shorthairs out for a walk. We were out in the grasslands south of the Grand Canyon – on the outskirts of the small town of Valle. The wind was blowing hard, bending the stalks of grass down almost to the ground, and the Shorthairs were enjoying the opportunity to explore and exercise. High in the air above us I saw some birds circling, and one seemed to separate and come spiraling slowly down – obviously watching the dogs. I began to get a little concerned, and I called the dogs in. Fortunately, Greta closed in on Annchen, my old brood bitch, as they both came in. It was a good thing they did because that little speck soon became identifiable as a Golden Eagle, who had obviously come down to assess whether our little pack offered an opportunity for a meal. He hovered in the wind perhaps a hundred feet above my head, paying little attention to me but focused intensely upon the pup. Annchen, however, was another thing entirely, and I think he rightly decided that it was poor odds as who would eat whom if he decided to try and take the pup. Knowing Annchen, my money would have been on her. Had Annchen not been there, however, I think that Greta would have been in grave danger indeed.

As we introduce a young pup to the field, we need to keep these things in mind. At eight weeks a German Shorthair pup may weigh ten to fifteen pounds – which makes it vulnerable to a variety of predators, other dogs, and livestock. When we start letting our pup go afield at this age, we need to keep safety in mind. I prefer to introduce young pups to the field in an open area, away from automobile traffic and other dogs, where there are physical barriers such as fencing to prevent a pup from running away. I like the area to have some weedy patches for the pup to explore – but for it to be open enough that a young pup won't have undue difficulty walking and running. I also want to be able to keep the pup under constant observation. High School athletic fields often offer such facilities.

At this age, what we are doing with the pup is building its confidence by allowing it to run and play – and laying the foundation for future cooperation in the field. We do this by transferring the lessons that the pup has been learning in the house and yard to the field.

In particular, this is the place to reinforce and practice the come command, and to practice retrieving. Remember that when a pup is dilatory in coming back (and all pups will get sidetracked by intriguing scents and curiosities), you need to move AWAY from the pup to trigger the pup's instinct to chase and be close to you. Having said that, the field should be a place for your pup to grow and build confidence. Let the pup explore, run, and play. In the wild, mama will allow the pups to play and explore under her protection and observation. When they begin to get too far away- at a distance where she would no longer be able to fend off a predator –she'll call them back in. When she does, she requires unswerving obedience –the pup's safety depends upon it. Like mama, we don't want to continually drill our pup into boredom and resistance. This is easy to do as pups have very short attention spans. However, when we do call – we need to make sure that puppy completes the drill and comes back.

Also remember that the distance at which a pup can explore safely will expand as the pup grows and becomes more physically capable. When the pup is eight weeks old, the circle of safety may only be ten or twenty yards. By the time the pup is six months old – that circle may be two hundred yards or farther.

Deference and Trust

I've talked about building a habit of deference in other sections, and perhaps this is a good place to explain the concept. It's actually fairly simple. As I noted before, because of our large stature and status as the food giver and physical master of the pup's universe – we automatically inherit the alpha status. The pup will naturally defer to us – subordinating its decisions and movements to ours. In the house and the field, the pup will follow us around, eat on the schedule we set, etc.

When I talk about building a habit of deference, this is simply reinforcing in the dog's natural perception that we are the leaders. To do this, we have to behave like leaders – and in particular the canine definition of a leader. Much has been written over the years about how to behave like an "alpha" canine leader – most of it focused on physical coercion. Advice about biting your dog's ear, or rolling it over and biting its neck, or thrashing your dog, or staring it down – seems to be all over the internet chat rooms. If you start by behaving as the leader right from the beginning, almost all of that will be unnecessary and irrelevant.

When you think of how to behave as the leader, and establish that habit of deference, think of yourself as a king or queen. That's the nearest thing we have in human society to a canine pack leader. Can you imagine Queen Elizabeth running after an underling to get them to obey a command? Or letting an underling drop off a package halfway rather than bringing it to her hand? Or allowing an underling to tell her where she will go and what she will do? The leader is the one who decides what is going to be done, where and when. That is your role. That doesn't mean that you need to be a rigid jerk. You can be a leader and still respond to your puppy's invitation to play, or pet your dog when he puts his head on your knee. However, this needs to be done in the context of a relationship where your leadership is clearly recognized, and the dog habitually defers to your decisions.

As we try and train our pup, our pup is also trying to manipulate and train us. Often it becomes unclear exactly who is training whom – and if you are having some issues with your pup it is useful to stop occasionally and ask yourself that question. Typically, this manipulative behavior is most prominent among pups and young dogs seeking to find their level in the pack – usually pups from the time you bring them home to the time they are out of their adolescence. The more that the pup can control our movements and actions – the higher the pup rises in the pack hierarchy. If we allow the pup to manipulate us and control our actions on a regular basis – we have a recipe for problems.

The problem is that we often don't recognize when our pup is manipulating us, or when we are deferring to the dog rather than the other way around. One good way to figure this out is to examine our movements in relation to the dog. If we are conforming our movements to those of the pup- chasing it to get it to drop a bumper or to reinforce the come command –the pup is calling the shots. Don't allow this. If your pup is routinely putting you through the paces, instead of vice versa, something is wrong with your basic relationship.

In the hunting field we will expect our German Shorthair to reliably hunt for the gun. Those habits are instilled early in a pup's life

Previously I mentioned that the way to get the pup to come was to move AWAY from the pup. In doing so, you use the pup's natural instincts to reinforce your leadership – you are the one determining where everyone is going and the pup is deferring to your lead. This is critical. In the hunting field we will expect our German Shorthair to reliably hunt for the gun – coordinating its movements with ours. We need to build this habit early on.

In addition to refusing to follow the pup's movements, we can refuse to defer to the pup and insist upon it's deferring to us by depriving it of attention. As a pup grows, and becomes able to outrun us, it will inevitably pull stunts designed to manipulate us into following its lead. This is natural and even desirable – but we need to resist these manipulations. The way to do this is to shut everything down until the pup comes back into compliance. If a pup is playing keep away with the retriever bumper – don't chase the dog attempting to get the bumper. Sit down, with your back to the pup, and ignore it. Pretend you are involved in something else. Eventually, curiosity will bring the pup over to investigate – and you can reestablish control by having the pup sit.

You are probably thinking that this isn't really asserting dominance – which is often viewed as forcing the dog to back down and grovel. Well, it isn't asserting dominance – it is simply being dominant. Leaders don't have to constantly force their underlings to obey – if they do they aren't very good leaders. As noted above, we are building the habit of deference on the part of our pup. Once the pup learns to trust your judgment, and is happy to follow your lead – you've established the basis for your lifelong partnership.

I've added the word trust into this section because it is integral to the relationship we're establishing. Those whose dogs have not developed a habit of deference, whose independence leads them to do what they want, are dogs that their owners will not be able to trust. These are the dogs you see in the hunting fields strapped down with electronic collars because their owners don't trust them not to run off.

At the same time, owners who have not exhibited regular leadership, but instead have relied upon periodic punishment to attempt to reestablish lost leadership, have shown little for their dogs to trust. Owners whose responses are erratic, who give unclear signals and impose seemingly arbitrary punishments, don't inspire trust in their dogs, they inspire anxiety.

Once we have our pup responding reliably to the come command in the field –we have to trust them to roam and explore. This is important to note: for a hunting dog trust is built first and foremost in the field. As we are teaching the pup the habit of deference – we are also learning to trust our pup. That, in turn, inspires our pups to learn to trust us. Once they learn that we will let them function naturally as our partner – without yelling at them or giving them unnecessary direction – they will pay greater attention to those commands we do give.

Trust is easy to claim, but harder to establish. With our dogs mutual trust is established by consistent behavior and repeated examples of trustworthiness. Most hunters work for years with their dogs to establish a level so profound that they often literally trust their lives to each other. We start on the path towards that level of mutual trust by learning that once we have taught our pups to come when called, we then need to limit our use of the command and give them the freedom to learn.

This is scary. Most of us worry that if we let our pup get out of sight, or out of our direct control, something bad will happen. They will run off and we won't be able to find them, or they will get lost and won't be able to find us, or all other sorts of bad things could happen. And with improperly socialized, independent dogs this is possible – but with well socialized dogs with whom we have built a strong bond, it is unlikely. The truth is that if we try and keep them constantly under our control and in sight at all times – that's when something bad is really likely to happen. A frustrated pup prevented from working as its instincts dictate will start to habitually disobey – and again we will have developed a relationship in which trust is absent. One more dog wearing a shock collar for the rest of its life afield.

While much of what really establishes mutual trust will happen as the older pup and adolescent spends time with us afield, at this preliminary stage we are laying the foundation. That foundation we are laying is a simple bargain: if the pup comes to us when we call reliably – then we will trust the pup to work away from us and not call it until it's honestly necessary. At two months, that will likely be when a pup hits that ten or twenty yard mark. At four months, however, a pup will often have been out of sight for a few minutes when we finally call. That is made possible by the confidence and trust we have built in our pup, and that they have built in us.

9

Puppy High School – Intermediate Training.

This stage generally takes place during late puppyhood – that period from four to ten months of age before canine adolescence really sets in. Again, this isn't determined by the calendar as much as it is by how well the pup has the training foundation outlined in the previous chapter, and whether the pup has the physical development to proceed to its intermediate training.

We should now have a puppy that knows and executes the four basic obedience commands, sit, stay, come and down; that is fetching and retrieving objects on command in the house and yard; that is holding a steady point on the wing on a string; and that is accustomed to walking afield with us. Training during the intermediate stage is focused on reinforcing the obedience lessons already learned; polishing manners; improving handling in the field, building a reliable retrieve from land and water; and transferring the pointing behavior the pup learned on the wing on a string to the whole bird.

As our pup has learned the basics of obedience, built a foundation of hunting behaviors, and learned the habit of deference – it has also grown in physical stature and confidence. The pup will have, or soon have, a mouthful of real teeth instead of milk teeth. It's coordination and strength have increased to the point that it can easily run and jump without stumbling, and its curiosity and boldness have increased apace. The pup is now capable of doing things that it physically wasn't able to do just a few weeks before. With this has come growing confidence to explore and learn, to test limits and boundaries, and to evaluate situations analytically. For the next few months the pup will learn at an amazing rate – absorbing knowledge like a sponge.

However, it's important to remember that pups absorb both bad and good knowledge at the same rate. This means that a lack of attention, or some casual thoughtlessness, can cause a pup to learn bad behaviors that we may spend months or even years trying to correct. The best way to avoid this is to ensure that you put the pup into situations where it can learn the lessons you want –and avoid situations likely to teach the pup bad manners. You want to think through the training situations and methods that you use to evaluate the possible negative affects, and minimize the chances that you will cause unintended problems. Again, this means that anger can have no place in your training. If you train angry you will almost inevitably wind up teaching the pup things that you don't want it to learn, and doing things that you will later regret.

Obedience II – Directional Commands:

To the obedience foundation that we built in the first phase of training – we are now going to add the directional signals that will give us the ability to exert greater control over our dog's movements in the field. We want to be able to do this for two reasons:

The first is safety – we want to be able to "steer" our dog away from dangers such as busy roads, livestock, traps, uncovered mine shafts and wells, and other hazards. Unfortunately, many of these hazards are surrounded by "birdy" looking cover that is enticing to a bird dog – and if we aren't paying attention they can easily lure our dogs into situations that can result in injury or even death.

The second is that, particularly with young dogs, I want to be able to "steer" my dog into areas that I believe hold birds. Some hunters claim that this is unnecessary because they can't find birds as well as the dog. This is a specious claim. I have been hunting desert quail (in some of the same places) for 35 years. I have learned more in that time about the biology and habits of desert quail than any young dog could possibly know, and I have better eyesight and a higher vantage than my dog. To say that I can't contribute to the day's hunt by directing my dog into areas that are likely to hold quail, or that I have nothing to teach a young dog, is just silly. Every dog should be trained to take directional signals.

Directional commands tell the dog in which direction you want them to head while in the field. These commands are primarily visual commands that are given to the dog with your body movements -although retriever trainers generally train these as whistle commands as well. With waterfowl directional commands are generally used to guide a retriever toward a downed bird that the hunter may have seen drop but which the dog did not.

Teaching a German Shorthair to obey direction signals is fairly easy. Most pointing dogs instinctively want to "hunt to the front." They key their movements to the hunter in order to cover ground ahead of where the hunter is heading. You can use this instinct to teach them to obey directional signals by simply stopping, getting the dog's attention by shouting its name or with a whistle blast, extending your arm fully and clearly to the right or left to indicate which direction you want the dog to go, and then turning sharply in that direction and walking. In order to keep in front of you the dog will naturally follow your lead and move ahead be hunting in front of you again. After some repetition, a dog will soon come to understand what the directional hand signals mean - though you have to make sure that you exaggerate them enough so that a distant dog can see them.

The directional signals precise enough to steer a dog to a downed bird, are trained somewhat differently. In this type of training, dogs are steered by "giving them a line" (pointing in the direction you want them to go) toward an object previously planted. When pups are young and starting out you might use bits of hot dogs to let them learn that when they follow a "line" that you give them something good will be at the other end. The dog learns that if they follow the direction precisely, they will wind up with a "prize." Once they've got the basic equation – then we usually move to a retrieving dummy or perhaps a frozen bird. Trainers vary this type of training by planting a number of different objects at differing distances and giving the dogs different "lines" so that they understand that they have to precisely follow the directions being given. Once a pup has learned to take a line – extending that training to the water is a simple matter of giving the dog a line to objects in the water at progressively further distances.

Field work – Intermediate

At this age a pup is getting to the point where it is physically able to work in the field at close to an adult dog's pace. It can easily work at a speed that will make it impossible for us to catch –and as the pup gets bolder – a speed that can take it out of sight in the blink of an eye. We are now at a point where the foundation we have laid by taking our puppy out afield with us will pay dividends. This is a good thing, because now that the pup is physically big enough to outrun us, and is bold enough to be comfortable ranging independent of us, teaching field manners would be a more challenging proposition most likely involving check cords and electronic collars.

By taking the pup on walks afield with us regularly when it is first able to do so –we are able to teach the pup that going afield is a regular occurrence. In doing so we have let the pup learn that obeying recall commands, and keeping touch with us in the field aren't negative things that result in a return to domestic imprisonment. Instead, they are simply part of a normal pattern that will result in more time afield in a day or two.

It seems counterintuitive in a way – but my experience is that dogs that are kept under near perpetual physical constraint in the field and close control by the handler when off lead are most likely to take advantage of the opportunity to run riot and ignore recall commands. A pup that believes that it won't have the opportunity to run afield again is the one that will be most inclined to find ways to extend the experience and make the most of its fun time – even at the expense of punishment at the end.

Our pup by this stage should be comfortable working in the field with us, should keep in touch with us naturally, and should be obedient to the commands it has been taught. At some point in the pup's early adolescence – the pup will challenge the status quo. Once it understands that it is faster than you are, and that your ability to catch it and punish it is near zero, it will wander off, either intentionally or unintentionally, and become "deaf" to the come command.

146

However it develops, this is an important point because it is most likely the pup is testing you. If you are in very thick brush – the pup might really be lost, and your shouting may in fact lead it back to you. However, if an out of sight pup, or one that was very recently in contact, hasn't returned within a few minutes – the likelihood is that this is another challenge. Once again, it is trying to see whether it can obey it's own inclinations and whims in the field, or whether it will have to conform to your directions.

In cases where you can see that the pup is ignoring the come command –either because it is refusing to acknowledge the command at all, or because it has acknowledged the command by pausing and looking at you but refusing to obey, you need to turn the tables again. At that point, once you are sure that the pup has heard the command but ignored it – stop giving the command and search for a bush or something that will hide you from the pup's sight, preferably downwind that will also keep your scent from him.

When the pup isn't looking, sit down and hide, without making a sound. Although the pup is busy showing how bold and independent it is by defying your commands, the reality is that the pup is still paying attention to you and wants the comfort of knowing where you are. Your brave pup really has no desire to be a lone wolf in a big, hostile world – he just wants to see if he can be the boss in the field. He doesn't want to lose you – he just wants you to follow him and do what he wants.

Once he's realized that he lost you – panic will begin to set in. He may stop and bark, if so don't move or give your position away. At some point, his panic will induce him to come back and search for you. When he does find you, greet him and reassure him (this will have been traumatic enough so punishment isn't necessary and is actually counterproductive), make him sit and come – and if he obeys then continue your walk. Once again, what we want him to learn is that failure to obey the come command will always result in tragic and scary consequences imposed by an all seeing universe. His ignoring the come command results in your disappearance – something few puppies really want to experience.

147

With most pups, it only takes one or two such occurrences before they respond reliably to the come command. Once this hurdle is overcome – work afield becomes simply a matter of building trust and teamwork. As the pup gets more comfortable in the field, it will naturally extend its range until it is working at a distance that is close to the edge of where it can keep track of you by sight, hearing, or scent. You need to learn to be comfortable with that.

Ranging Afield

A cooperative traditional German Shorthair will work naturally as part of a team – coordinating its movements to yours. At the same time, we want our dog to range out in order to cover a wider area than we alone could cover, find and point game. While the balance between these two somewhat contrary requirements is determined by each dog – in general the German Shorthairs tend to find a happy medium. A traditional German Shorthair will tend to work at ranges of anywhere from 50 to 300 yards depending upon the cover and terrain. The German Shorthair will tend to work at closer ranges in forested or broken country where keeping in visual or aural contact with the handler is difficult, and tend to stretch out in more open country where it can see or hear the handler at greater distances.

Newcomers to pointing dogs, or those who have only had retrieving or flushing breeds, often get nervous about dogs that range beyond gunshot. This is inappropriate for the German Shorthair and other pointing breeds. Their job is not to flush birds within range of the gun, but rather to range out, find, point and hold birds for the hunter to flush. Attempting to artificially restrict a German Shorthairs range to within gunshot is inappropriate – you need to have faith in your dog.

This faith extends to the other aspects of your dog's work afield with you as well. One of the keys to maintaining a habit of obedience and deference in the field in your dog is that you don't give your dog unnecessary commands. It can be unnerving when a young pup first begins to explore out of sight –and like any nervous parent the impetus will be to call them

German Shorthairs are strong natural retrievers. Training should focus on polishing what's already there.

back. However, as with parenting, it is a mistake to try and keep the pup tied to your apron strings. Before recalling a pup that has wandered out of sight, wait a few minutes to see if the pup will check back in on their own. Nine times out of ten they will – if you just have the patience. Remember, after five minutes even a pup that has drifted out of sight and been working away from the hunter at a normal pace will still typically be within a quarter mile or so– within normal voice recall range.

Constantly calling your dog back, or giving it directional signals either limits its initiative and independence, or just annoys it. Simply put, it's nagging. If you want your dog to respond reliably to commands in the field, those commands should be rare. In the field, I can go for hours without commands other than those needed to call dogs in for water and health checks. The partnership between a good experienced German Shorthair and hunter becomes so intimate that they reach a point where they know what the other is thinking and coordinate without needing verbal communication. The foundation for this type of relationship is laid during this training period, so it is important to start as you mean to continue –without undue hacking and giving your pup the benefit of the doubt.

Retrieving phase II

At this point the pup should know that fetch means that we want it to go out, pick up a designated object, and bring it back to us. The ball of socks we have been throwing for the pup in the house and the yard has taught it the basic command and desired action. Most German Shorthairs love to do this. I can throw a tennis ball for most of my dogs until my arm falls off, and they would still be enthusiastic about finding and retrieving the ball. One of the great advantages of the German Shorthair as a breed is that the retrieving instinct is still so strong. So, typically, our job in terms of teaching retrieving at this stage is two fold – we want to transition our retrieving to the field so that our pup is comfortable retrieving objects in a variety of natural situations, and we want to introduce the pup to water and retrieving from water.

When the pup was small, we used objects that it could pick up and carry easily to teach it to fetch. Now that the pup has grown, we can move on to larger objects that are closer to bird sized, and are rugged enough for use in the field. As noted above, the first object I move to is the tennis ball. It is easy to throw a distance, large enough to detect fairly easily, fits easily in a dog's mouth, and floats. The transition from the rolled up sock to the tennis ball is easy and requires little more than switching the one for the other.

Once the pup is eagerly retrieving the ball in the house, and in the yard, we will transfer the activity to the field. We want to take the pup to a large, relatively open area free of vehicular traffic or excessive distractions. The first retrieves we ask the pup to do should be fairly easy – throw the ball underhand in relatively open terrain so that the pup can easily see the ball while telling the pup to fetch.

The pup will typically perform these retrieves like a champ – chasing down the ball and bringing it back. However, at some point you will encounter two issues that will need to be addressed. The first of these is that at some point the pup will stop and attempt to play keep away with the ball. This is a pup trying to get you to play, but under the guise of play it is

When the pup gets old enough, I switch to a training dummy for retriever training. The retrieving foundation laid at this age will pay off in the years to come. Photo courtesy of Margaret Cotton.

also the pup changing the whole retrieving dynamic. DO NOT LET THE PUP FAIL TO COMPLETE A RETRIEVE IN THIS WAY!! The remedy for this is simply not to allow the pup to take over the training.

If the pup stops short and refuses to complete the retrieve order the pup to come in a severe stern tone of voice. You want the pup to know that this isn't play and that you aren't happy – but you don't want to be screaming like an idiot either. Remember, in dog talk a low growl is the most serious sound there is, while higher pitched loud vocalizations usually accompany play. Feel free to growl if you feel so inclined. At the same time, turn and move AWAY from the pup. We want our back to be to the pup, and we want it to follow us as we move. When the pup comes up, we want to stop, have the pup sit, and then give the ball. By having the pup sit, we are reestablishing our status and control. The pup must conform its movements to your directions or it is not obeying and you are not the leader.

If the pup still doesn't want to come into compliance, and continues to try to play or otherwise refuses to deliver the ball then we need to do two things. If the pup is within hearing, you can try the sit/stay command to reestablish obedience. This command will often get through to pups who are disobeying the come command – and bring them to their senses.

If this doesn't work, then you need to shut the whole thing down. Sit down on the ground with your back to the dog. Remain quiet. Do not engage with the dog – you are letting the dog know at this point that you will not let it dictate what happens and that you will not play with it. Keep your back to the dog –even if it moves to get into your line of sight. This is a test of wills. At some point, the dog will come over to you to try and get you to play. When it does, take the ball from the dog's mouth, put the dog on the leash, and fold everything up. Do this without any sound. Remember, anger rewards the pup with attention – just as chasing after it does.

The reason that we so obviously refuse to engage with the pup in its play under these circumstances is that we are teaching the pup that we are the boss, that we control the daily activities of the pack – and that we won't play the pup's games at its bidding. The pup needs to learn that failure on its part to complete the retrieve doesn't get rewarded by a game of keep away and watching the human humorously run about and shout. Failure to play by the rules means that the game's over.

The second issue we encounter is short stopping – where the pup drops the ball short instead of delivering it to hand. This is usually a pup simply trying to take a short cut by dropping the ball off short and then getting in better position to intercept the throw that it knows is going to come. In the field on birds the motivation to drop the bird short is to try and get back to hunting and finding more birds. Some hunters don't mind this – as long as the dog retrieves the bird to within easy range of the hunter they don't mind walking over and picking it up. I think it's sloppy and I insist that my dogs retrieve to hand.

I do this by the simple expedient of not accepting anything other than a delivery to hand. If the pup drops the bird or bumper short I point to it and tell them to fetch it up. The game doesn't resume until the pup brings me the ball. At this point the pup should know that the drill includes a retrieve to hand, so it knows what you want. Don't accept anything less. If the pup won't pick the ball up and bring it to you – then leave it on the ground and walk away from it. Nine times out of ten the dog will pick it up and bring it to you in an attempt to get another throw. If it doesn't, then shut down the exercise – you can always get another tennis ball. If you want your pup to sit to deliver to hand as some hunters do, give it the sit command before accepting the ball – and insist that it always do the sequence properly before you throw the ball again.

As the pup becomes more adept at retrieving the ball from open ground, I then tend to try to make the retrieving tasks more challenging. I'll throw the ball into cover where the pup can't easily see the ball on the ground to teach it to search with its nose. Typically, I will toss it into increasingly thick cover – the kind where a wounded bird can be almost guaranteed to land – to teach the pup how to search cover for the object to be retrieved.

Because of the size of the pup's bite, I mentioned that I typically move from a rolled up sock to a tennis ball as my retrieving tool. As the pup grows and becomes more reliable at retrieving – I then move to a canvas covered training dummy. I do this specifically so that I can secure two bird wings to the dummy with a wrapping of duct tape. I want to get the pup used to the feel of feathers in its mouth, and to searching for the dummy by the smell of feathers/birds. At some point, a pup will usually try and stop and start plucking the feathers off of the bumper. This is a natural instinct that I want to catch and discourage. A stern NO! is usually enough stop this – and hopefully keep the pup from doing the same thing to a downed bird.

Hard Mouth

Given the hound heritage of the German Shorthair, many Shorthairs are prone to what is called "hard mouth."

153

Technically, hard mouth is when a dog bites down on a bird during a retrieve to the degree that it breaks the skin and mangles the bird. However, hard mouth has come to be used to refer to any sort of mouthing or biting during a retrieve that adversely affects the quality of the game as human food. Some Shorthairs give a bird a quick "chomp" to ensure that it is dead and not likely to scratch them or escape. This is particularly true of Shorthairs that have been spurred or scratched by wounded pheasants – many automatically deliver a killing bite before they bring the bird back. Others tend to roll the birds in their mouth, covering them with slobber. I personally am fairly tolerant of many of these behaviors – as long as the skin isn't pierced and bones aren't broken I'm comfortable.

Obviously, hard mouth is undesirable in a dog that is retrieving game we hope to eat. If your pup shows signs "hard mouth," chewing or biting down hard on the dummy, I will switch to a new, clean scrub brush with stiff bristles. I tape a wing to the back of the brush and throw it as I would the dummy. The stiff bristles poke the roof of the dog's mouth when it bites down hard, teaching it to carry the dummy without chewing or biting. Wooden backed scrub brushes will float so they can also be used for water retrieves. With young pups this can be all it takes to teach them to handle their birds with delicacy. As the pups get a bit older, I will have them retrieve whole frozen game birds – which gives me a better idea of how they will really deal with a bird in their mouth. If the pup seems inclined to chomp then I'll move them to the "balloon game." This is where we use a small, inflated, balloon as a dummy for the pup to retrieve. Adding some water to the balloon before you inflate it will make it easier to throw, but requires that you work with the pup outside.

I tend to like the small, narrow balloons that clowns use to create balloon animals because when inflated they are still small enough in diameter that a pup can easily get its mouth around it. You want to try and get the balloon to the point where it is well inflated but still has a little give. The idea behind the balloon is that we want our pup to find out that if he bites down too hard, the balloon will pop and end the fun. However, we don't want a balloon so full that it's pop will scare

Typically, German Shorthairs love to swim and getting them to take the plunge takes little more than giving them the opportunity. Photo courtesy of Margaret Cotton

the pup out of retrieving balloons at all. With timid dogs I will often just use water balloons to avoid that problem. It may take a few tries, but usually a pup that's a chomper will learn how to carry and retrieve the balloon without bursting it. At that point, it may tape a couple of wings to the side of some balloons, plant them in the yard, and send the pup for retrieves. If the pup is as delicate on the balloons with feathers on them as with the others – we have likely solved our hard mouth problem.

Water

Typically, German Shorthairs love to swim and getting them to take the plunge requires little more than giving them the opportunity. However, some pups require a little encouragement. If you have older dogs that swim well – taking the pup to the pond with the rest of the dogs and letting them learn from the grown ups is probably the simplest and easiest way.

If you don't have other dogs to show the pup how fun swimming is, then we can encourage the pup to swim by taking our retrieving game into the water. For a pup that retrieves the ball/dummy with zest, then we can start water retrieves by taking the pup to a calm pond or lake that is free of underwater hazards or natural threats, and tossing the ball into the water close to shore in water that is easily waded. This may only be a foot or two at first.

Once the pup is comfortable going into the water to get the ball, then toss it a little bit further out. Eventually we want to get it into water just deeper than the pup's legs that will require that the pup swim to get the ball/dummy. Often a timid pup at this point will whine and give you accusatory looks as it sees the ball bobbing just a foot or two beyond it's reach. With some encouragement, at some point, the pup will break down and swim to get the ball. Once this happens, and the pup learns that it can swim without harm – teaching water retrieves simply becomes a matter of repetition. I should also note that while you can use this method to teach the pup to swim while you are based on the shore – it is more fun for all concerned if you can do so on a nice warm day while you are in the water yourself.

Pointing – the transition to birds

Once the pup is pointing staunchly and reliably at a wing that it can't see – and is physically developed enough to work safely in the field – it is time to take the pup's pointing to the next level. Remember, we used the wing on a string to lay the foundation for pup to point birds. The puppy has learned that finding things that smell like birds is fun, that it will generally have to use it's nose to find them, and that when it does find one it needs to freeze on point.

Typically, this makes the transition to work on real birds quite easy – most pups make the transition without any problems. However, for this transition to occur requires birds. For most hunters who live in suburbia –this can pose problems.

The best way to bring your pup to the next stage is by exposure to wild birds. It is worth traveling some distance for the opportunity to put your dog on wild birds. The reason is that wild birds are the ultimate teachers for a bird dog. They will not tolerate mistakes, and the lessons they teach a young pup are all good. A young pup is unlikely to catch a bird unaware on the ground, or snatch it out of the air – as is so common with pen raised birds. The type and level of scent a wild bird puts out is not tainted by human smells and the smells of birds crammed artificially close to each other. In fact, exposure to wild birds is so important that no dog can be considered a true hunting dog until it has had such exposure and proven itself on the "real deal."

This is why it is worth taking extra efforts to take your pup afield in areas where it is likely to encounter wild birds. You need to check and make sure that you do so at a time and place where local game laws permit such work. Many states forbid disturbing game birds during the nesting season –and even if they don't waiting until the chicks are old enough to be able to easily evade the dog without harm is just common sense. The event most likely to cause us problems at this stage of training is having our pup catch a bird on its own – getting the opinion that it no longer needs us to complete the cycle that results in a dead bird in its mouth. Typically, this is rare occurrence with wild birds that daily have to face the threat of sudden death from foxes, coyotes, hawks, owls and dozens of other predators. However, it is much more likely to occur if the pup encounters newly hatched chicks whose ability to fly is limited. So waiting until chicks are not such easy prey is not only good conservation – it's good training sense as well.

Many pups will transition to birds so seamlessly that they wind up pointing birds staunchly from their earliest exposure. However, at some point most pups will make an effort to attempt to catch a sitting bird. Some pups just believe they can catch a bird if they can get there quick enough and they start out as bird bumpers. Others start out pointing and then break. The temptation of having a bird sitting inches in front of its nose just proves too much. The great thing about wild birds is that they will teach the pup the lesson it needs to learn about breaking and rushing – that it can't catch the bird and that it needs me, the hunter, to get the bird in its mouth.

157

When the pup charges birds, we need to let it know that what it's doing is bad – so I verbally chastise a pup that bumps and chases birds. We don't want to overdo it – and make the pup afraid of birds in the process. We simply want to cuss the little reprobate a bit to let it know that these antics are not part of the program.

Many hunters don't have access to populations of wild birds, and are forced to use pen raised substitutes. Typically these are bobwhite quail, chukar, or pheasant. The problem with using such pen raised birds is that they are weak flyers and generally behave unnaturally. To a dog, such birds smell like sick or crippled birds – and the urge to rush in and grab them is much stronger. I can always tell when my dogs are on point on pen raised birds instead of planted birds because their tails flag a bit on point whereas on wild birds they are as stiff as a poker.

These problems are one of the reasons that many trainers prefer to use homing pigeons for training – they fly much stronger and tend to be tougher than planted game birds. However, as "dark meat" birds they also smell different and many dogs dislike them. While pigeons are stronger flyers, they are also often easier for a dog to catch than wild game birds. Having your dog catch a bird is the primary thing you want to try and avoid at this stage–so you should structure they way you use pen raised birds accordingly. Use release traps and fly the birds well before the pup is within pouncing/jumping range. It isn't the end of the world if a pup catches a bird – but it is an irritation that will cause training problems and set your pup back.

That they can't catch the bird themselves is the one core lesson that every pointing dog needs to learn – and they learn at varying speeds. Some pups may not get it for weeks – others will learn the second or third time they try. When they do break and chase the bird – you should verbally chastise them, though not too harshly. It is not a bad thing that the pup is doing this – it is part of the learning process. Most pups have to go through it. What is bad is if the pup continues to do this long

Baretta points in the Grouse woods. Photo by Cindy Stahle

after it should have learned better. Letting the pup know that it is doing bad without being so harsh as to make it associate the birds with chastisement is the tool we use to help reinforce the undesirability of this behavior.

One aspect of this that is very important is that until your pup is pointing staunchly without hitches or backsliding – *you should never shoot a bird in the field that your pup didn't point properly!!* If you need birds for the pot and the pup isn't pointing properly – put it up and hunt yourself. You don't want to teach your pup that it can get a bird in its mouth without first pointing it for you. Once this lesson is firmly established –then you can pick up those accidental flushes. Until then – accept that you are teaching your pup more than you are hunting.

When the pup figures out that it can't catch the bird and starts to point staunchly – that's when you have a hunting dog. We refer to it as the point the light comes on – that magic moment when a pup has reasoned through the whole process and recognized that its job is as part of a team and it understands it's role. It is one of the great moments in a dog's life, and in a dog owner's life. If I think about it, I can remember the moment the light came on for every one of my hunting dogs for the last twenty years – which isn't bad for a fellow who has trouble remembering what he has for breakfast. It also shows what a wonderful, magical thing this really is. That's why you need to remember to praise your dog and let them know how wonderful they are when that moment comes.

159

Whoa

Over the past forty years American pointing dog owners have been bombarded with the message that all pointing dogs must be whoa broken in order to be trained. Most US training books, magazine articles, newsletters and blogs start with this premise. This has become training dogma in the US, and is rarely questioned. Even the thought that a dog may be able to turn into a fine Pointer without being whoa broken is heresy. However, this dogma is only held in the US. Other countries, including Germany where the German Shorthair was developed, don't teach whoa as we know it here. As they have been turning out trained pointing dogs for a lot longer than we have it begs the question-why have Americans gotten so hung up on training whoa?

The answer quite simply is that the majority of our most well known professional dog trainers have traditionally been associated with horseback field trial dogs rather than hunting dogs. Since horseback field trial dogs are judged primarily on how fast and far they run – this is the aspect that breeders tended to focus on. As a consequence, the natural pointing instinct in many strains became subordinated to the urge to run –and trainers needed to find a way to train such dogs to point. They developed a method of training that required that a dog be taught to whoa – or halt – instantly upon command and to stay frozen in place until released.

Once the dog has learned to whoa on command, the dog is introduced to birds in a controlled situation, and given the whoa command when it first scents the birds. The dog soon begins to associate the smell of birds with act of stopping – and learns that it is to freeze when it gets bird scent. This method can effectively teach dogs with little or no natural pointing instinct to point. In fact, an enterprising British nobleman once taught a pig to point using such methods. All things considered, it is an almost perfect method for training field trial dogs.

However, where a dog has strong natural pointing instincts not only is whoa breaking unnecessary – it forces the dog and handler into an adversarial relationship that is frustrating for both. It can also require a degree of force such as hanging dogs, choking, balancing them on barrels, etc. that I personally won't use. When I first started training my dogs, I whoa broke them with all of the headaches that entailed. However, I soon came to realize that this was an unnecessary step that –since I don't train my dogs to be steady to wing and shot – taught them nothing of long term value. I was trying to force them to go through an artificial training regime to get them to do something they wanted to do naturally. I found it was much simpler just to let the dog's instinct provide the point.

Some proponents of whoa also argue that it is a useful safety command – but I haven't found it to be so. In 35 years in the field I have never once used the whoa command, or felt the desire to use the whoa command, in a safety situation. In dangerous situations I almost always want my dog retreat from danger and come to me –and where I don't the sit/stay command works better to fix a dog in place. If you don't have to use whoa to teach a dog with little natural pointing instinct to stand birds – then the only reason I see to teach the command is to help train the dog to be steady to wing and shot.

Introduction to the Gun

Until about ten years ago I had never even seen a gunshy German Shorthair. All of the Shorthairs I knew had taken the introduction of the gun in stride. However, about a decade ago I rescued a one year old pup that my Billy had sired. Trudy had been bought by a gentleman who had intended to hunt her but never seemed to find time to interact with her. He put her into a kennel in his back yard and basically left her out there for a year with little contact with humans or other dogs except for a once per day feeding. The one thing he did with her was to do exactly what every book says you shouldn't do – he took her as a small pup out to a trap and skeet range and tied her in the back of a pickup while hundreds of shots were fired. When I picked her up she was starved for affection, thoroughly neurotic, and completely gunshy. As a consequence, she never became a hunting dog –though her father was the best hunting Shorthair I've ever seen.

161

I do think that there are genetic components that can make a dog timid and unsure which may make them prone to gunshyness – but I agree with most trainers who say that it takes a human to make a dog gunshy. They do this either intentionally or unintentionally by putting the pup into a situation where the gunshot has no context –and the noise and blast is simply a source of fear and stress.

There are many techniques outlined in training books to introduce the pup to the gun and help it avoid gunshyness. Some advocate making progressively louder noises when the pup is fed – banging pots or shooting off cap guns. Others involve holding a pup on lead and then firing off small caliber weapons at a distance – moving progressively closer. I've always found these techniques to be overly complex and unnecessary – and perhaps likely to backfire. I know of one fellow with a timid pup who made it so nervous with loud noises that it routinely threw up its dinner.

From my perspective the best way to introduce the pup to the gun is in a safe situation where it's attention will be on other things, not on the shot. I introduce pups to the gun in the field, in the company of older dogs who are comfortable with the gun. The situation is set up to make the shot a matter of the lowest concern – vastly overshadowed by the joys of working a field, playing with other dogs, and finding and chasing birds.

Once we have the pup comfortable working in the field, and comfortable working with us – I make an assessment of the pup's mental state. I want a pup that is enthusiastic about going afield – and which has grown enough mentally not to be timid or halting in the field. A pup that is bold in the field is less likely to pay much attention to a shot. As added insurance, I bring along older hunting dogs who know all about the shotgun, and can be relied upon not to flinch.

I don't do anything special with the pup, such as showing it the shotgun, because I want this to be a normal trip to the field. I don't want the pup sensing that something is amiss or unusual –so I don't behave as though it is. When we arrive at the field, I unload the dogs, and then grab my vest and shotgun as I would if we were hunting. We head afield and typically the pup will run alongside and play with the older dogs. A windy day is best for this exercise as it serves to diminish the impact of the shot. I also would advise not to use a training area where the shot is likely to echo, or its affect magnified. So canyon areas, hollows, or areas bordered by tall mountains should be avoided.

There are two ways to actually fire the first shots over the pup. British authors advocate having an assistant downwind that fires the first shot away from the pup at a distance of perhaps two hundred yards or more from the pup. Then as the pup gets used to the sound, they move the shotgun progressively closer. This method works and is perhaps a safer way to deal with pups that might be a little timid.

With bolder pups I wait until the pup is well away from the gun (at least 100 yards) and engrossed in it's business and then I fire off a shell away from the pup and keep walking as I would normally. I shoot away from the pup because the concussion can be a big part of what scares a small pup. If the pup comes running over for comfort or attempts to jump up – I ignore it. The whole message is that this is something completely normal-like a cricket chirping – not a reason for fear. The older dogs should be giving this message as well. Most pups will soon learn to ignore the sound of the gun, and as birds are shot will come to associate the gun with birds to retrieve.

However, if the pup seems to be unduly scared by the gun – stopping what it's doing in mid stride and hightailing it back to me with it's tail between its legs – I won't fire another shot. Remember, there is no need to rush this process –if the pup isn't yet ready for the gun, firing off more shots will not make it ready – it will only scare it further. While I don't want to acknowledge the pup's fear because I then reinforce it by giving it legitimacy – I also don't want to make it worse. However, if the pup simply pauses, looks about with some confusion or alarm, and then, after seeing me continuing to walk and the other dogs ignoring the shot, goes back to playing and searching – the pup is learning what we want. I will then wait another fifteen minutes or a half hour – until the pup is

A pup should learn to love, not to fear, the gun. Whether that happens is up to the hunter

thoroughly engrossed in doing what it's doing – before I fire another shot. The period of alarm this time should be shorter – and if it is I repeat the process until the pup doesn't pay any attention to the shot.

At this point, I have successfully introduced the dog to the gun. However, it's important to remember that you can still make a gun broken dog gunshy by doing something spectacularly stupid. Shooting over a dog's head while it is sleeping or otherwise not expecting the shot, shooting from inside a car while the dog is also inside, tying it out at the trap range, and other similar bonehead actions can turn even the bravest pup into a sissy where the gun is concerned. Even though the pup has become accustomed to the gun, you still need to use common sense. A young pup should be brought along at a steady pace –each day's training reinforcing the last. It should not be metaphorically pushed into the deep end and asked to sink or swim.

10

Dealing with the Bumps in the Road.

At this point we have a young pup that will retrieve from land and water, that will point and hold its birds, that is accustomed to the sound of the gun, and that reliably obeys commands in the field. We have this whole gun dog training thing sewn up, right? Our pup will now perform flawlessly in the field for the rest of its life, right?

It would be nice if this were the case, and sometimes it is the case, but for the vast majority of pups there will be further hiccups and we will need to reinforce various aspects of training at some point. Again, it is important that we remain the leaders of our pack, and that we continue as we mean to go on –not accepting backsliding or sloppiness

The terrible twos

In the canine world, adolescence is just as big a pain in the butt as human adolescence –for the same reasons. Hormones are cooking, physical changes are taking place, and psychological changes are taking place. Because this period typically falls during a pup's second year – from about 10 months of age to 20 months of age depending upon the pup – it is colloquially called the terrible twos. It is a period when a young pup is challenging for its place in the pack hierarchy, exploring its new physical abilities, and often making poor decisions. Sound familiar?

Not every pup has significant problems during this phase. If you have a pup that continues to learn its lessons, hone its skills in the field, and reliably obey you during this period – thank your lucky stars. More likely, your pup will at some point test you and the rules you have set up – making it clear that it believes it can do what it wants and be damned to you and your rules. The important thing to remember when your lovely pup has eaten a hole in the kitchen drywall for no particular reason, stolen the thanksgiving turkey from the counter, and seemingly forgotten everything it has previously learned in the field, is that this too shall pass. If you can avoid killing your youngster for the next six to twelve months – your pup will regain its sanity once it matures. Patience, often the patience of a saint, is the proper response to the terrible twos.

Having said this, as with teenagers, you need to maintain structure and boundaries for your pup during this period. Pups should not be allowed to get away with their testing –or you will lose authority. In a canine pack such testing is typically dealt with by growling, posturing, bared teeth, and ultimately biting if the pup won't back down. Those dogs who back down to the pup lose status – and you don't want to be one of those dogs. However, you don't want to have to be constantly threatening or biting your pup either. There are some simple tips that will help get you through this period.

In most cases you can reestablish authority by going back to the most basic commands – the ones that are naturally and instinctively most likely to be obeyed. The most prominent of these is the sit command. If you have a pup that has suddenly turned deaf, that is obviously ignoring you or disrespecting you, command it to sit in a severe tone of voice –and once it has sat then give it some other commands before releasing it. By showing it again that you are the boss – you have dealt with the challenge and further violence or force is not necessary. Remember, once a dog has come into compliance – physical punishment is not appropriate. We don't want the pup to learn that compliance and obedience results in negative consequences.

Social ostracism is also an effective punishment for adolescent dogs. Even though these pups are challenging the rules and pushing for status – they still want very much to be a part of the pack. Giving a pup a time out by putting it in its crate in a social setting – where it can see the family's activities but not participate – is an effective punishment for most infractions.

For adolescent dogs that seem to forget what they learned in the field – the best training tool I have found is jealousy. Adolescent dogs will not limit their challenging and testing to your home – it will also show up in the field. Typically it will show up in deliberate bird busting, selective deafness, or refusing retrieves or playing keep away. When you have a dog that you know understands what it is supposed to do, but suddenly stops doing it without any obvious reason for doing so – you can be fairly confident that you are dealing with the terrible twos.

Perhaps the best way to deal with such issues is through the use of the "chain gang." The chain gang refers to a long chain that professional trainers typically stake out when training to which they can tether a number of dogs at the same time. Those dogs that are not actively training are able to watch the other dogs go through their drills. In terms of the trainer training their own pup – the chain gang just refers to putting a pup aside in a place where it can watch an older dog successfully complete the tasks that is failed to do.

If I have a dog that's being a boneheaded teen – refusing to retrieve, or busting birds – I'll put them in a controlled situation and allow them to fail if they choose. Again, we are talking about situations where a dog has stopped doing something that it was doing before, and clearly understands how to do. So if we are having trouble retrieving – we'll go back to a bumper retrieve and do some controlled retrieves. When the pup fails –either through refusing to make the retrieve or in failing to complete the retrieve – I stop the action, put it on a lead, and either tie it out or put it in a crate where it will have a good view of what comes next. I will then bring in an older dog that I know will reliably complete the drill, put it through the drill, and conspicuously praise it upon the successful completion. I'm trying to make my bonehead jealous. When I can hear from the crate that my teen is green with jealously – whining and scratching to get out and be part of the action – I'll put the older dog up and bring out my pup to do the same drill. Most of the time, the pup will complete the drill properly –and when it does I will lavish it with praise to let it know that all is forgiven and that I haven't abandoned it for that interloper. If the pup still fails – I'll put it up again and repeat the process. It typically doesn't take more than two or three times for even the biggest bonehead to break and complete the drills properly. The message you are giving the pup is that if it doesn't want to play by the rules and do its job right, you can always find another dog that will and the pup will sink in the pack hierarchy. This is the worst possible message a pup striving to rise in the pack hierarchy can get.

Manners while on lead – the prong collar

Along with the other issues related above, the growing physical strength of the adolescent German Shorthair can pose problems with control while on a lead. It seems it's almost as common to see a German Shorthair on a leash dragging its handler around the neighborhood as it is to see a handler in control while walking their Shorthair. Shorthairs are strong dogs whose pulling power has actually made them the favorites of some dog sled racers. Once a young dog gains it's full strength - enforcing manners while on the lead can take some time and effort.

Many trainers recommend the use of a choke collar in this situation – but choke collars actually don't work very well and can easily harm the dog. Most German Shorthairs I know are perfectly willing to choke themselves silly pulling against a choke collar if they can get closer to something that interests them. A more effective tool for dealing with this kind of pulling is the prong or pinch collar.

The prong collar is a gruesome looking chain collar that looks something like a medieval torture device. It typically consists of two strands of chain connected by half to one inch prongs that stick up toward the inside of the collar. While this looks gruesome, in fact the prongs are not sharp and are designed to imitate the feel of teeth on a dog's neck – not inflict pain. In a dog pack the way an alpha enforces discipline against an offending dog is by putting it's teeth on the dog's neck which causes the dog to cease struggling. A dog that pulls against a prong collar while on a lead gets the same sensation and naturally ceases its offending activity. If you watch a dog being walked with a prong collar you'll note that it will not pull against the collar as it will against a choke collar – and it is actually a fairly humane tool with which to teach a dog not to pull. Like any tool, it can be abused – but in comparison with a

The e-collar can be a valuable tool in the hands of a skilled trainer. In the hands of an amateur it can be a disaster.

choke collar I feel that the prong collar, despite its appearance, is the more effective and humane.

The e-collar

This book may be a little unusual for an American hunting dog book in that it doesn't base its training upon the use of the electronic collar. Thanks to decades of marketing by e-collar manufacturers – many American hunters have been conditioned to believe that an e-collar is a necessity for a hunting dog. The truth is that while the e-collar can be a valuable training tool-it can also cause significant damage. I suspect that for every dog trained successfully with the collar – there is a dog that was ruined by it as well.

The e-collar is neither inherently bad nor inherently good. In the hands of a skilled trainer with the ability to rigidly control their temper – the e-collar can be a very valuable training tool. It gives trainers a reach and flexibility that they haven't had before. It is particularly useful in aversion training – in teaching our dogs to avoid dangerous things such as snakes or porcupines. Indeed, it is likely such training would not be possible without the e-collar.

However, there is something inherently risky in using a device that allows us to cause pain to our dogs simply by pressing a button –without needing to pause for reflection. In so doing it offers the potential for instant gratification for our frustrations and temper – without regards to the effects on the dog being trained. This is dangerous. Training and handling dogs is an inherently frustrating activity-and even experienced trainers can lose their cool. Having the ability to press a button and inflict pain on a dog under such circumstances is an enormous temptation – one that if indulged can cause tremendous harm to the dog.

Too many people press that button not because they think that doing so will enlighten or teach the dog, but because it is an angry impulse that allows them to vent their frustration and anger. All of the blinkers (dogs that avoid birds because they associate them with negative experiences) that I've seen were created by fools using e-collars. Many of them weren't even aware that they were causing a problem until they found that their pointing dog was now avoiding birds instead of pointing.

It takes knowledge, patience and force of character to use an e-collar properly – and given the ability of the e-collar to cause problems so quickly, those who don't possess those attributes are better off not trying an e-collar.

Aggression

I debated putting this section into this book because the issue is so rare with German Shorthairs. While they are a courageous breed, they are not a breed that is typically aggressive towards humans. In World War II German forces used German Wirehaired Pointers and Weimeraners for guard duty – but they didn't use German Shorthairs because they were considered too friendly to humans. However, since aggressive dogs, no matter how abnormal, can show up in any breed – I thought I would include these remarks in the event some unfortunate individual has to deal with the issue.

There is one area where I will respond with substantial physical force to a pup/adolescent during its formative period and that is where a dog exhibits strongly aggressive actions toward people. Any young pup/dog that starts growling at people, baring its teeth, raising its hackles, snapping, or otherwise physically challenging me or members of the family is going to get what it would get in a dog pack – an instant and thorough thrashing. Indeed, in a wolf pack such behavior is so unacceptable that the pup exhibiting it, if it doesn't back down, will be killed or driven off. If once you let this behavior take hold, if your dog learns that it can make you back down by threatening you, you will never be able to trust it.

Such aggressiveness will almost always start to show itself in two areas – around food and toys, and when the dog is being forcibly displaced (particularly where it has been sleeping). Any dog that growls and snaps when you attempt to touch its food bowl or toy, or which growls and snaps when you order it off of the bed or couch – is exhibiting unacceptable aggressive behavior. I respond instantly by grabbing the dog by its collar and holding it off of the ground – strangling it for long enough for it to get the message that I could easily kill it should I desire to do so. If that doesn't do the trick, I will thrash it with a leather leash until it clearly yelps and cries. With pups I will grab them by the scruff of the neck and yell at them. I think that I have had to do this with only two dogs in 35 years with German Shorthairs – both were rescues who had been abused and psychologically damaged.

However, in doing so I believe that I saved one of these dogs from being euthanized (the other had already been driven so hopelessly psychotic that it had to be put down)– and that is what we are really talking about here. Statistics show that half of the children in the United States will be bitten by a dog before their 18th birthday. Some will be killed. An aggressive dog that is not afraid of humans is a menace that can not be dealt with by simply trying to pawn it off on some person that lives in the country away from people. It will always be a danger – and if you can't fix the problems by an early response and/or effective behavioral conditioning, the dog should be put down. That's why it's important to respond to these things early –before they become fixed patterns.

11

Hunting with your German Shorthair

Years ago most hunters who hunted over pointing dogs were brought to the sport by their fathers or grandfathers. The knowledge of how to hunt with a pointing dog, how to read a dog, and how to work a dog through different types of terrain was passed from generation to generation. The same demographic trends that took Americans off of the farm and into cities and suburbs also took many of us away from that tradition. Statistics show that many if not most of those who are purchasing German Shorthairs today as hunting companions did not grow up hunting over pointing dogs. Some are taking the plunge because they have hunted with friends or acquaintances with German Shorthairs, others because they have seen hunting shows on television with pointing dogs and decided to give it a try, still others because they have read and researched before they decided that a German Shorthair was the dog for them. In any case, this chapter is dedicated to those who are new to the sport of hunting birds and waterfowl with their German Shorthair – and contains some tips that even experienced hunters might find useful.

Using the wind

The first thing to understand about hunting with a pointing dog is that, as in sailing, everything is determined by the wind. The dog locates birds by scent – and to scent the birds at a distance it relies upon the wind and breezes to bring scent to its nose. In good scenting conditions a German Shorthair with an excellent nose can scent birds more a quarter mile away. In order for this to happen, the hunter has to put the dog in a position to pick up bird scent carried by the breeze. This means that the dog and hunter have to either work into the wind, or across it. Having the wind blowing at the hunter's back and the dog's rear handicaps the dog and doesn't allow it to use its nose to best advantage.

Hunter and dog achieve a level of human/canine cooperation rarely seen elsewhere.

Dogs that work into the wind will typically make long curving runs called casts to either side of the direction of travel. This enables the dog to cut across the breeze and not only scent those birds that might be directly in front of them, but also birds that might be hiding a hundred yards or so to either side. Essentially, when a hunter and dog work into the wind in moderately open terrain they are scanning a swath two to three hundred yards or more in width with the hunter in the middle. Birds within that swath should be detectable by the dog in normal scenting conditions.

Dogs that work across the wind will typically run far to the front and then work back to the hunter. These dogs too are working a swath of terrain that extends from the hunter to as far as the dog runs forward, and then anywhere from 30 yards to 400 yards to the windward depending upon scenting conditions.

The ultimate objective of hunting in these types of situations is to minimize the time that hunter and dog spend with the wind at their backs. Hunting with the wind to the dog's back handicaps the dog and helps minimize its effectiveness. So when you are first approaching a hunting area – it pays to think a bit about how the wind is blowing and how you and the dog can most effectively work the area to work the cover and take best advantage of the available breezes.

For example, let's suppose a hunter wanted to work an agricultural field that was a mile square with plots of cover scattered throughout, and the wind was blowing from east to west. Entering the field at either the Northwest or Southwest corner would be the best choice. The hunter could then work a long zig-zag pattern a little east of south to a little east of north that would have it and the dog working across the wind. Ideally, the hunter would want to arrange it to that the dog passed by as much of the likely looking cover as possible on the downwind side, so that the breeze could bring the scent of any hiding birds directly to the dog. They could then work back to their vehicle in roughly the same way. While hunting situations are rarely so cut and dried, this example gives a good indication of how a hunter can work an area to maximize the chances of success.

Sometimes you don't have much choice about how you work terrain given limited access and inhibiting barriers. It's either follow this route or not at all. However, most of the time there is some discretion about how to work an area with the dog, and the hunter that stops to give it a bit of thought and works the terrain to maximize the dog's chances of picking up scent is the one that will find more birds.

Nose

For a number of years I worked for the United Nations and the United States government putting together programs to remove uncleared land mines from countries around the world struggling to emerge from the aftermath of conflict. It has long been recognized that one of the best tools for finding buried land mines is a dog's nose. Dogs are so good at detecting explosives that their scenting ability has been widely examined and analyzed by military research facilities in various countries for decades. In fact, the US military has been working to develop an artificial dog's nose for mine detection – a detector as sensitive as a dog's nose but which could operate in hostile terrains that would be dangerous for dogs. Many of the explosives detectors in modern airports have their roots in this research about dog's noses.

Military research from various countries has given us the best scientific information to date about how a dog scents things – and it is pretty amazing. The first thing that the military research tells us is that all dog breeds with normal nasal passages (not pug noses) have roughly the same physical ability to gather and process scent. They can detect things literally down to the molecular level – differentiating tiny samples of one type of molecule from all of the others. We need electron microscopes to do the same sort of differentiation. Dogs are now being used not only for finding explosives and drugs, but for finding tumors in humans and detecting other human maladies. Indeed, a dog's ability to scent is almost a superhero level power.

So why do certain dogs find birds when others can't in the same place and conditions? The truth is that Nose as we call it isn't a physical attribute, it is a mental attribute. While all dogs have noses that can gather and process scent at a roughly similar level – they differ widely in the level of concentration at which they will react to that scent. So Pointer A might get birdy when it hits concentrations of 100 bird molecules per million of air – while Shorthair B might get birdy when it hits concentrations of 50 bird molecules per million of air. Both dogs have scanned the air with equal ability – but it is the processing and reacting to the information gathered that gives the Shorthair the better nose in this example.

Over the years we humans have selectively bred various domestic dog breeds to react to scent in different ways. We have given some dogs such as blood hounds and pointing dogs relatively low thresholds at which they recognize and react mentally to scent. We have given other breeds such as Rottweillers or Greyhounds much higher scent thresholds because scent would distract from the jobs we want them to do.

The German Shorthair has one of the best noses in the pointing dog world. While this ability varies from dog to dog – traditional German Shorthairs are known for their excellent

German Shorthairs are known for their excellent noses and ability to scent birds - even under hot, dry conditions.

noses. The care that the original breeders took to infuse the breed with the superlative scenting qualities of tracking hounds has remained an integral part of the breed. Indeed, this remarkable nose is one of the characteristics that have made them the most popular pointing dog breed in the world.

Scent

If we have defined the tools that a dog uses to locate birds at a distance as nose, then scent is the other half of the equation. Scent is the trail or residue of molecules that a bird emits as it goes about it's daily activities. The lighter of these molecules travel on the breeze for some distance, and are picked up as air scent by searching dogs. The heavier of these molecules stay lower to the ground and don't tend to get blown around as much. We refer to this as ground scent.

In optimal conditions air scent streams away from the birds in a long cone of scent – like a plume of smoke drifting in a slight breeze. A dog can pick up this airborne trail of scent while moving at a fair pace and follow it back to it's source –

the bird. However, if you ask any experienced hunter what constitutes optimal scenting conditions – you'll never get an absolute. Most of us believe that cool, moist air with a moderate breeze constitute optimal scenting conditions. The cool temperature keeps the dog's nose from getting overheated and inflamed, the humidity helps carry scent molecules and keeps the mucous membranes of the dog's nasal passages moist, and the moderate breeze serves to carry the bird's scent to where the dog can easily locate it. Having said that, I can point to numerous days under these exact conditions where I've seen the dogs have obvious difficulty scenting birds, and hot, dry days where the dogs seem to know each bird's exact location.

In less than optimal conditions it is typically the air scent that gets lost to the dog. Either because it is dispersed by strong winds, or bandied about by capricious breezes, or washed away by too much humidity, or baked out of the air by too little humidity – air scent seems most affected by adverse climactic conditions. Under these conditions ground scent – that scent that lingers near the ground just below the tops of grasses and bushes – is generally more reliable. It is not as easily dispersed by the wind – nor displaced by humidity or its absence. Unlike Pointers and Setters, which have been bred, to use air scent exclusively to find birds, German Shorthairs have been bred to use both air and ground scent as appropriate. This ability gives the German Shorthair and extra advantage when working in adverse scenting conditions – as well as making it a highly competent tracking dog.

While we know that birds put out scent that is picked up by dogs in certain ways – there are times when birds just don't seem to put out scent. Nesting hens and cocks on the nest seem to put out almost no scent at all. This helps protect them from foxes and other nest raiders. In addition, birds that have flushed and flown for a distance are what are called "air washed." They seem to have the scent washed off of them – and even the best dogs will typically have difficulty in locating a bird that has been air washed. It's common to see a dog that hasn't accurately marked a fallen bird have extraordinary trouble finding even those that are right under their feet. Birds that have flushed and set down can also be almost invisible to a dog's nose – for a while. Typically I have found that waiting ten minutes or so to give the birds time to put out scent will once again enable the dog to find them. This works on downed birds as well as live birds that have settled into cover.

Having said all of this, the truth is that there is still an element of magic about the scent a bird puts out and the way a dog is able to locate and process that scent. We use smoke as an example of how to envision scent moving – but we know that it actually doesn't move in an exactly similar manner. It's just the closest example we have. We also know that there doesn't seem to be any absolute rules – only generalities that are true much of the time. So the best advice I can give is to play the odds – work the wind and the terrain to try and give your dog the best possible chance to encounter scent, and then trust your dog to find it.

Range

Perhaps no aspect of how a pointing dog does it's job is more controversial than range. Many writers give the impression that a dog that isn't running to the horizon, that isn't making casts of a quarter mile or more, doesn't have the fire to be a first rate hunting dog. These writers are simply parroting field trial lore – lore that doesn't seem to understand the difference between running and finding birds. For an upland hunter, finding and pointing birds is the most important role of a bird dog – the aesthetic satisfaction of watching a fast dog run can be left for the greyhound track.

There are a few things that need to be said about range. The first is that it is genetic. A dog's range is programmed into it by its genes. To a large extent this range is a function of where the pup's personality falls between the spectrum of cooperativeness and independence. Dogs that are programmed to be cooperative, to work as part of a pack, maintain close contact with the hunt leader. You will rarely see wolves working a half mile or more from each other. Dogs that are extremely independent have no reason to maintain close contact with others. They are lone wolves hunting for themselves.

Over the eons, humans have taken advantage of these personality tendencies to develop specialized breeds that function in ways most effective for the type of hunting they wanted to do. Retrieving and flushing breeds tend toward the cooperative side of the spectrum because hunters have no need for dogs that flush birds a half mile away or more from the gun. Instead, they have tended to breed these dogs for their cooperative nature –which makes them tend to stay close to the hunter/pack leader in the field, to be more biddable, and to be naturally inclined to retrieve. While some of the retriever field trialers have been heading in a different direction in their breeding and training – in general the rule holds true.

On the other hand, owners of pointing dogs have little reason to have a dog that works within gun range. This defeats the purpose of having a dog that will locate and point game – allowing the hunter time to come up for the shot. Instead, pointing dog hunters want their dogs to range out and search cover terrain that they themselves are not able to cover. They have therefore tended to breed dogs that move more towards the independent end of the spectrum than the retriever breeders. By increasing the independence and search range of pointing dogs hunters have multiplied the amount of land that a hunting dog/hunter team can cover. The question is how far towards the independent edge of the spectrum do you push your breeding given what you lose in terms of cooperation, how you increase the frequency of unproductive points, and how you increase the tendency towards self hunting?

To a hunter, that answer depends upon the terrain and type of game birds being hunted. Can a dog that routinely runs far and fast effectively cover broken terrain or thicker cover? The answer is no – a dog that has its focus on running hard and making half mile casts is not effective searching area where scent cones are broken and interrupted by brush, trees, ridges, and arroyos. At the same time, while bobwhite in the past would hold docilely under point for extended periods of time – most of the game birds that hunters are hunting today will do so only for a short period of time. My friends who are bobwhite hunters are telling me that nowadays even bobwhite seem more inclined to run out from under point than they did in the past.

As a result, this tends to reduce the question of range to something of a mathematical formula. While the tendencies vary from bird species to bird species, the amount that birds have been hunted, and the quality of the cover – species such as pheasant, desert quail, Hungarian partridges, and chukars in my experience start to run out from under point after about five minutes and rarely hold longer than ten minutes under point. So if you figure out how long it will take a hunter to walk to a point in the terrain they are hunting – you have a good rule of thumb about the maximum range you want your dog to work. In open prairie, where a dog is easily visible and a hunter can move quickly – that distance might be a half mile assuming a hunter's average walking speed of 3 mph. In more broken country that distance will shrink to 200 - 250 yards assuming an average hunter's walking speed of 2 mph and some slippage for the time it takes a hunter to locate the dog. In heavy cover such as the grouse woods or woodcock woods – that maximum range will shrink to probably 75 to 100 yards given an average hunter's walking speed of 1 mph, and additional time to locate a dog on point in conditions where visibility is limited.

Dogs that run bigger than this tend to lose game and often run beyond the distance at which a hunter can keep track of them. Hunting behind such dogs can be an exercise in frustration. The number of unproductive points, where no bird is found in front of a dog's point, dramatically increases with such dogs. This is why so many questions that I get asked by newer hunters have to do with adjusting a dog's range. The vast majority of these hunters want their dogs to hunt closer – though I occasionally get a question about how to extend the range of a close working dog. What I tell them is that each dog comes programmed with a natural range, and that while moderate changes may be possible – such changes generally come at a high price in terms of hunting effectiveness.

One of the methods that is often advised to bring in a dog's range is to work the dog in a training field where the birds have been planted close to the handler. The idea is to get the dog to associate the handler with the presence of birds – so the dog will always pay extra attention to searching the vicinity around the hunter. My experience has been that such dogs soon learn in the field that the presence of the hunter is no guarantee of birds, and begin to revert to their natural range.

The other method often used is to put an electronic collar on the dog and to shock it if it ranges beyond a certain range. This can be effective as long as the dog is wearing a collar – the minute it is taken off the dog is typically off to its natural range. However, I believe this also comes at the expense of some of the dog's hunting effectiveness as it splits the focus of the dog. Not only is the dog's brain focused on finding birds, it is also focused on not ranging as far as its natural predilection in order to avoid being shocked. This keeps the dog from focusing it's entire faculties on the hunt –with a consequent diminishment in hunting effectiveness.

As difficult and minimally effective efforts are to decrease a hunting dog's range, efforts to increase range are typically even less effective. For a dog whose close range is due to a strong cooperative nature, a handler can sometimes achieve moderate increases in range by increasing the distance at which a dog can easily maintain contact. Singing – allowing your dog to maintain contact with you at a greater distance by hearing you calling or singing to it in the field is an old trick used by grouse field trialers. In more open country a hunter can increase range by hunting their dog off of horseback – which allows the dog to see the hunter at a much greater range.

For a dog whose close range is due to timidity – typically because of a bad experience the dog encountered while ranging farther away from the hunter – time will often help heal these wounds. In my experience, these problems are often caused by a ham fisted hunter with an e-collar who shocks an unwary dog at a distance. However, these can also be caused by natural trauma such as a dog that was bitten by a snake when working at range, or stung by wasps and hornets, or injured in other ways. Such dogs stay close to the handler for reassurance and a feeling of safety. As the dog regains its confidence, it's range will typically extend by gradual increments – basically to the limits at which the dog feels safe working away from the hunter. Any steps that a hunter can take to increase that feeling of safety, from taking the dog to work in areas different from that where the trauma occurred, to taking off the e-collar, to simply having patience and behaving in a reassuring manner – may speed along the psychological healing process.

READING YOUR DOG

Dogs can talk – don't let anyone tell you otherwise. And German Shorthairs are as communicative as any. I don't mean that they speak actual words – though my Billy can vocalize at least a couple of dozen different messages to me. I mean that they can communicate with us clearly and precisely – describing what's happening, asking for advice, telling us what we need to do, and otherwise exchanging information and points of view. We just have to learn how to understand what they are saying to us.

In the wild, dogs have highly sophisticated non-verbal languages that they use for both social and hunting purposes. I recently watched a documentary on wolves in Yellowstone that showed four wolves driving away a full grown male Grizzly bear (that easily outweighed all the wolves put together) from an elk they had killed. They could not have done that without sophisticated coordination that insured that the bear always had at least one wolf biting it from behind. The language that dogs use with us as hunters is easily as complex.

I'm using language in the broadest context when talking about the communication between dog and owner. At its most developed it can be so intimate and marked that it almost looks like ESP. Even basic communication can have this appearance because most of the communication between a hunting dog and hunter is based upon body language. The complexities and subtleties of canine language are such that entire books can be written on the subject (and have), and there isn't space here to address this topic in tremendous detail. Instead I'll describe some of the basic ways that my German Shorthairs communicate with me in the field and at home – which I hope may help you learn to better read your dog.

With his raised ears, body posture, and stiff, upright tail Billy is telling me that moving birds are right ahead

The Tail:

The tail on a dog is like a semaphore – it's various positions and motions signaling a wide variety of information. I find German Shorthair tails particularly easy to read because of the docking and shorter hair. I find that the extra length and flowing hair on other breeds can make it hard to read more than the basics – though hunters more used to those characteristics may be able to read them better than I.

Dogs communicate in two ways simultaneously with their tails, by the tail movement and the tail position. We all know that a wagging tail held at normal tail level is a sign of joy. A wagging tail held high is a sign of cautious greeting to a newcomer that might prove to be an enemy. A wagging tail held low and tight is a sign of submission and a desire to placate. So you can see that the simple act of wagging a tail can convey a number of different messages.

Tail language gets even more complex when we start talking about a German Shorthair working in the field. The tail clearly expresses the dog's thoughts. A working German Shorthair that is covering ground will typically wag their tail at a relatively leisurely pace as they run. As their nose captures scent, their tails will reflect the type and strength of the scent. If the scent is of something that you don't hunt – such as fur or vermin – it will increase the rate of wag, but at a subdued level. If the scent is bird scent, the rate of wag will typically increase significantly, and get faster the closer the dog gets to the bird. If you see a dog exhibiting interest in a scent on the front end and a tail going like crazy on the other – that dog is "birdy." As the dog gets quite close to the bird –the tail will slow down and get more subtly expressive before locking up on point. A stiff tail moving with deliberate slowness indicates that the dog is connected to a bird that it hasn't yet pinned. Either the bird is moving, or it hasn't yet been located exactly. Once you and your dog have handled a few birds, you'll soon learn to differentiate between the two. A ramrod straight tail held with such tension that you can almost see the sparks flying from it indicates that a bird has been pinned. A point with a tail that is held without the high level of tension and rigidity usually means a point on fur, a non-game bird, or a pen raised bird. A point with a tail that goes from rigid to flagging or less tense indicates that it is unsure about the presence of the bird. Some dogs give this sort of point for a minute or two before jumping in on a wounded bird for the retrieve. Most hunting dogs will flag – wag their tail very slightly on point – when confronted with pen raised birds, indicating their disdain for such sickly prey.

After you've been around your dog for a while, paid close attention to it's tail mannerisms on game in various situations – you will soon learn your dog's language. My Billy, for example, can tell me with his tail what type of prey he's tracking, how close he is, whether the birds are nervous or calm, whether the birds are moving and how fast, and when he has birds finally pinned – all with his little tail.

The tail is one of the most expressive parts of a Shorthair. The stiffness and position of this tail is confirming that Annchen has a bird pinpointed.

Ears:

After the tail, perhaps the second most physically expressive part of a German Shorthair is its ears. German Shorthairs, because of their size, shape, and hang have particularly expressive ears. Raised ears combined with a questioning expression typically indicate curiosity. Raised ears that are skewed to one side or the other indicate that a dog has detected a sound and is trying to determine its location. You can usually determine the basic direction from which the noise is emanating by the position of the ears. Ears held low and close to the head can indicate fear and aggression – or submission depending upon the circumstances. A dog on point that has a bird pinned will typically have raised "alert" ears.

Body Posture:

This one is hard to describe in a concise manner because a dog has a great variety of different body postures that indicate a whole variety of things. Walking stiff legged with hackles raised indicates a swaggering, threatening posture. This is a dog looking for someone to back down or fight. On the other hand, stiff legs with a slow, tentative pace and intense focus is called catwalking – which typically occurs when a dog is following walking birds, or when a dog is trying to get closer to a wary bird that is holding tight. A dog that freezes on point for a short time, unfreezes and moves forward, then freezes on point again is dealing with running birds. A smart dog will try and hang back, maintaining contact with the birds, until they reach cover in which they feel safe enough to attempt to sit and hide, and then move in and pin the birds under point. A dog that points, walks, points, and then runs around quickly in a search pattern is a dog that lost the scent of running birds. A dog that cocks its head to one side is querying or trying to puzzle something out. There are literally dozens of different combinations of body postures that you will learn to interpret if you pay attention.

Eyes:

They say that the eyes are the window to the soul – and that same description can be applied to our German Shorthairs. Their dark honey eyes are incredibly expressive – and can draw forth instinctive human reactions. I can feel eyes boring into the back of my head as I type this - eyes in the skull of a German Shorthair that is trying to convince me to give it a dog biscuit. Not only can the intensity of a dog's gaze tell us something, but the size of it's pupil can also tell us a lot about it's mental state. These changes in pupil size make the dog's eyes look different to us in different circumstances – a subtlety that we can't always identify but which we can recognize. Eye direction is also a signal that dogs often use, looking from us toward a hiding bird or other object.

What these examples should show is that dogs communicate with us in a myriad of often subtle ways, and we need to pay attention in order to learn how to "read" what they are telling us. Doing so is one of the cornerstones of building a lifelong relationship. Learning to read your dog will not only make you a better hunter, it will make you a better dog owner.

Wild Birds and the German Shorthair

There's an old saying that birds make the bird dog. When we are talking about wild birds, this saying is certainly true. The relationship between the dog and bird is a wonderful and mysterious thing, and no dog can become a true hunting dog without experiencing that relationship. Pointing that first wild bird is a rite of passage for a young German Shorthair.

Given that a dog's nose has the ability to actually differentiate between molecules, working like a sort of long range scanning electron microscope, we can see that the scent based interaction between the dog and bird is extremely complex. Under optimal scenting conditions a dog can determine not only the type of bird, but also its health, it's mental state, its age, and a host of other things about the bird simply through scent. A dog that freezes on point is not just smelling a bird, it is scanning that bird and determining it's next moves based on the information derived from that scan.

A dog gets a remarkably precise "picture" of what's going on with a bird from his nose. Dog's noses are so sensitive that they are picking up things like the respiration rate, adrenaline levels, ph balance, altered body chemistry, etc. of individual birds. Essentially, a dog in good scent conditions will get a lie detector readout on the bird that it's pursuing.

With such information and the experience to process it, a good dog can perform remarkable feats. A good friend of mine called the other day to brag about his 19mo old dog who carefully followed a running sharptail for 500 yards before pinning it under point for a final, successful shot. Shorthairs routinely perform such amazing feats. I can honestly say that my Billy has gone entire seasons without bumping a bird - out of literally hundreds of birds pointed.

The reason for this remarkable level of performance is that through experience these dogs have learned to "read" all of the complicated information they are getting from the bird, to analyze it, and adjust their actions accordingly. Burton Spiller, the dean of American grouse hunters, called this the "Golden Thread" between the bird and dog. Among other things, it tells a dog exactly how close it can get to a bird without flushing it wild. They know this almost to the inch. I can't count how many times my dog stopped on point well away from a nervous covey that held tight for the dog, but flushed wild the minute I stepped closer than the dog's nose. This scent based connection tells them how close they can follow a running bird without forcing it to flush wild –and how to hold back to enable a bird to find cover and hold fast. The ONLY way a dog can learn how to handle birds like this is by doing it. They have to learn to decipher and interpret the scent they are getting, and to do that they have to make mistakes and bump birds.

Some hunters believe that they can avoid having their dogs bump birds by insisting that they lock up on point at first scent, and not move until released by the hunter. While this may involve some fairly fancy training – a dog trained this way will never learn to handle birds as well as one that is allowed to use its brain. Without the knowledge hard earned in the field of how to handle birds, it will bump birds and lose a lot of birds that run out from under point.

Wild birds are the ultimate teachers of German Shorthairs and other bird dogs. Dogs can be trained and run on all sorts of pen raised birds, but they are not accomplished hunting dogs until they can handle their wild birds. And the only way to learn to handle wild birds is through experience. Such experience is the canine equivalent of a college degree – wild birds teach the fine skills a bird dog needs to know in order to be an accomplished bird dog. There is almost no pointing dog problem that they can't solve, or help solve. The following story helps illustrate this point.

Billy and I had driven almost an hour and a half over dirt roads to get to our spot. When this story took place, Billy was a two year old German Shorthair, a beautiful dog, and smart as a whip. I kept him and his sister Rosie out of the only litter I had with Annchen. Both Billy and Rosie were proving to be outstanding bird dogs. Rosie was the quicker learner, and was already staunch on point and an excellent retriever. Billy was

Billy's day out. A couple of quail before lunch.

coming along slower, but had the physical makings of the kind of German Shorthair you see in your dreams.

This morning was his first day of college.

Billy was enjoying this boy's day out. His mom normally sat in the front seat of the Explorer – as befits a queen – and he and his sister rode in the back seat. With the whole car to himself he couldn't figure out where he wanted to sit, and so spent half the trip in the back seat, and after a rest stop, the remainder of the journey up front. As we bounced along the bumpy dirt roads, he watched everything with an eagle eye. Every so often he would whine pleadingly, as if to say "this looks great boss, let's stop here." When we finally turned off the main road onto a little track that ran a ¼ mile from the edge of a shallow canyon Billy could hardly contain himself. I smiled as we stopped and I opened the back door and let him out. He had been trying so hard to be good when every molecule of his being was exploding with pent up energy – like a little kid trying to be good on the drive to Disneyworld, worried that Dad and Mom might change their minds if he were bad .

Billy ran around and did what dogs do after an hour in the car while I put on my hunting vest, loaded up with a gallon of water, and pulled out the shotgun. After a quick drink of water

191

for both of us, we headed toward the edge of the arroyo. Billy was actually behind on his training on wild birds because the 1997 season (his second) was the worst quail season for forty years in Arizona, and 1996 hadn't been much better. As a consequence, I had not been able to put him onto many wild birds. The previous year, in 1996, I had introduced him to preserve Pheasant, and at 8 months he was a hunting prodigy. He was staunch on point and eager to retrieve.

However, the 1997 season proved to be a different story. He was a bit older and more full of himself in 1997, and began thinking that maybe he could do this hunting thing by himself. Added to this was the fact that finances prevented me from putting him on too many birds, and he got to the point where he was beginning to ignore or forget his training. Finally, after a couple of tries, Billy disgraced himself and all of his ancestors by bumping and catching a plump ring neck pheasant. Once he figured out he didn't need me along, he spent the last two months bumping birds as he tried to rush them after his point. He knew better, but discipline and scolding didn't seem to have any impact on him. He became Billy the Bird Bumping Bonehead.

In the off season I worked hard on getting him to steady (freeze) on command, and he got so good that he would slide to an immobile stop out of a full run if I yelled steady. However, once a bird was involved he got selectively deaf and ignored all of the commands. He even ignored a long check cord – lunging against the collar to get to the bird. I was at my wits end with Billy – so I decided to turn his case over to the experts. I knew that the true lesson on why he needed me along, and why he needed to remain solid on point, would be taught best by wild birds. They can explain this to a dog better than any human trainer and there are no better, wilder teachers of such manners than Gambel's quail. This trip was Billy's first trip to the school of bird dog hard knocks.

For those who have never hunted Gambel's quail, there are no tougher game birds to hunt in North America. They live in one of the harshest climates in the world, surrounded by efficient and intelligent natural predators. To survive they have to be tough, resourceful, and smart. When a Gambel's covey is feeding, they post sentries to watch for danger. If the sentry warns them in time, they quickly run into cover that usually is covered with spines. Most of the time you'll never know they were there.

We were still a couple of hundred yards away from the edge of the arroyo when Billy first locked up on point. I was surprised because it was an area of open land covered sparsely with grass and interspersed with Mesquite bushes - not area in which I would normally have expected to find Gambel's quail. I waited as he catwalked up, looking for all the world as though he were walking on eggs and trying not to break any. From his demeanor I could tell that the quail were moving, and that he was trying not to push them so hard that they would flush or run away.

I must have followed him for fifty yards as he stopped and started, pointing then catwalking, before he finally stopped for good. I could tell by the absolute immobility of his tail that he believed the birds were close. If he were going to jump in and bump the birds, this was the time he would do it. As I walked around to flush the birds, I kept waiting for that awful pounce, but it never came. He held as staunch as a statue, completely hypnotized by the scent emanating from the quail.

I came up to the Mesquite bush towards which he was pointing, and kicked at the base of the bush. Instantly, six Gambel's quail burst out - looking and sounding like tiny gray helicopters. Fast helicopters. I picked one from the group, one that was heading almost straight away, and then fired. It fell and lay motionless about twenty yards away. I then picked out another quail curving away to the right, and pulled the trigger instinctively. It arched behind a Mesquite bush about thirty yards away.

At the first flush of the birds, Billy had taken off after them, waiting for one to fall. When it did, he was right on it. Gambel's hunters traditionally allow their dogs to begin a retrieve at the sound of the bird's flush in order to enable the dog to get to the bird as quickly as possible. They believe that this helps recover crippled birds that would otherwise have quickly run into pack rat dens or impenetrable cactus thickets. Billy's performance was a good advertisement for the soundness of this belief. By the time I looked up after downing the second bird, Billy was halfway to me, a young Gambel's quail carried gently in his mouth.

After I took the bird, he raced off to find more quail to point, but I called him back. He came back reluctantly - his whole attitude one of exasperation. "But Dad, there's more birds out there - I just know it." "I know," I said to him, "but first things first. There's another bird down here and we need to find it - find the bird." At the sound of the last order, his ears perked up and he began racing toward the area I indicated, nose to the ground. As he quartered carefully through the area in which I saw the second bird drop I saw him freeze on point for a second, then pounce on something. As he turned around, I could see he found the second bird. After he had delivered it to me, I let him go down into the canyon.

The Southern slope of the canyon was covered with catclaw and thick grass - ideal Gambel's cover. Sure enough, he had only gone into the catclaw thicket about forty yards when I could see his tail start to wag frantically back and forth like a crazed metronome. He was on birds. A few yards beyond that, he froze on point. As I struggled through the catclaw after him, the heavy cordura facings on the legs of my brush pants were all that made it possible for me to walk through that patch without shredding most of the skin off of my calves. Sure enough, the small covey decided to flush at the most inopportune moment for me - a trait annoyingly common with Gambel's quail. I was only able to pick off a lone straggler. I was able, however, to mark where most of the covey had landed. Billy didn't see the dead bird fall for some reason, and I had to call him back to help search for it. Incidentally, for those who were wondering, the shade of gray on the feathers of a Gambel's quail are almost the exact shade of gray of a catclaw bush. Billy finally found the dead bird resting in the branches of a catclaw bush that I must have walked past and stared at five times.

We worked through the catclaw patch down to the bottom of the arroyo, where I called a temporary halt. I wanted to give the singles a chance to settle into cover and put out some scent. I pulled out the water bottle in my Game bag, and squirted a stream into Billy's mouth. He drank about half a liter of water before he turned away. Then I drank about the same amount. I then pulled out my hemostats, and began checking him for cactus quills. Most dogs learn fairly quickly about cactus, and soon learn to avoid them. However, when a dog gets a snootful of bird scent, such niceties are put aside. I don't believe my Shorthairs even feel the sting of the cactus spines when they are on birds. Therefore I make it a practice to regularly check my dogs for cactus spines every half hour or so when I give them water. Billy was fairly clean, with only a few Prickly Pear spines stuck into his front legs. I quickly pulled them out, and felt for the small golden spines that usually accompany the larger bone colored spines. When I found a clump, I would carefully pull them out with the hemostats. Billy thought this was much ado about nothing, but I didn't want him to develop an infection because of something as silly as cactus spines.

By this time, it was close to noon, and getting pretty hot. We worked down to the stock tank at the end of the arroyo, where Billy plunged in for an enthusiastic swim. Nothing cools a hard working bird dog down quicker than a good swim. As he swam and frolicked I found a shady Live Oak tree overlooking the tank and sat down. After a few minutes, my thoroughly wet Shorthair decided to come up and join me, and deciding I was way too dry, shook off about a gallon of tank water on me. Fortunately, I carry an all purpose bandana for these types of emergencies, and was able to clean off my bespattered glasses. Billy lay down in the shade beside me, and we listened to the wind in the trees and watched the clouds race across the sky for another fifteen minutes. I was astonished and very pleased by how staunch he had been on point so far, but I knew the real test would be hunting the singles. We headed out for the small ridge where I saw the covey that we flushed set down.

The ridge was one of a number of rust red fingers cut out by the washes that drained into the main canyon. It was probably only a quarter mile long, and a hundred yards wide, but it had plenty of grass and cover. The wind was blowing across the ridge, which was ideal for us. By starting at the bottom and working the crest of the ridge across the wind we were in a situation where the wind would bring the scent of quail in the draw and up the slope of the ridge right to Billy's nose. Sure enough, we hadn't gone more than thirty yards when Billy got birdy and headed down into an area thick with bunchgrass and prickly pear. Then at the base of a clump of bunchgrass he froze into a classic point, left paw raised daintily while his whole tense body pointed toward the BIRD!! Two Gambel's quail rocketed out of the clump when I kicked it, and I managed to drop both. Billy found both birds, and brought them back to hand with hardly a feather ruffled.

This set the pattern for the next hour or so. That ridge was covered with single birds holding tight in the heavy grass. Billy handled them like he'd been doing it all his life. In the next hour or so he made ten fine points, and I dropped seven birds. Each of these he unerringly found and brought back. I was overjoyed at his performance. Last season this perfect dog had been a perfect devil - chasing pheasants and chukars like a crazy fool. Now, he had made the transformation from hooligan to gentleman almost by magic. In thanks, I cut the day short, and we headed back to the vehicle three birds short of our limit.

I have to admit I wasn't really surprised at the transformation because I had seen it before in other dogs. In fact, I had brought him out alone hoping that this would happen. There is some special magic between bird and bird dogs, predator and prey, that is beyond our comprehension. They are yin and yang, linked together in the cycle of nature. Anyone who has ever seen a dog on point knows that the bird and dog are linked by a force so strong it is almost physical. Though we flatter ourselves about the effectiveness of our training methods, in the final analysis I believe that birds are what really make a bird dog. Birds teach a dog how to point and hunt, and wild Gambel's quail are some of the best teachers. Dogs instinctively treat them with respect. I was particularly thankful to them this day for teaching Billy his manners because I love him so dearly. He is a big, beautiful, sweet tempered dog that has all of the elements - conformation, nose, desire, temperament, intelligence, and toughness. All he lacked was manners. That was the gift those coveys gave him that day. I came in the morning with a bird bumping bonehead

of a teenage Shorthair - I left that evening with a Gambel's dog.
He's been a good one ever since.

This is why a good rule of thumb for those training German
Shorthairs is to always try the dog on wild birds before you
decide if you have a problem or not. Often the wild birds can
solve any potential problems before they can be realized. There
is nothing bad that a wild bird can teach a German Shorthair –
only respect.

SELF RELOCATION

There are two schools of thought about the way in which a
dog is expected to behave after first establishing point.
Traditionalists and trialers maintain that a dog should not
leave point until it is released by the hunter. They claim that
such discipline is necessary to prevent a dog from rushing after
birds and flushing them wild. These are the same folks that
train their dogs to first stop on scent, and refuse to allow their
dogs to behave in any manner outside the strict parameters set
by field trial rules.

Such hunters value aesthetics over substance. Years afield
hunting over dogs trained not to self relocate, and those that
are permitted to relocate, has taught me that dogs trained not
to self relocate regularly lose running birds. Gambel's quail, as
one example, have been clocked running at 15 miles per hour
in rugged terrain. In the five minutes it might take a hunter to
come up to a dog locked on point to release it, birds such as
Gambel's quail will have put more than a mile of distance
between themselves and the dog and hunter. Under such
conditions, the likelihood of the dog picking up their trail again
and pinning them down is virtually nil. Moreover, the worries
they have about dogs bumping birds are caused not by dogs
using their initiative, but by dogs being trained not to use their
initiative and so no knowing how to handle their birds.

As you can tell from the story above, I belong to the second
school on the subject of self relocation. The school that believes
that you need to let a dog use its judgment when handling a
bird, and that the dog should be allowed to relocate as it sees
fit. Because a dog knows much more about the state of that

bird at that instant, it should be the one to make the decision on how to handle the bird. And should a young dog accidentally bump such a bird, it gets the ability to learn from its mistake. A smart young dog will learn so quickly that it will rarely make the same mistake twice. Hunters should allow their dogs to learn to handle birds well, and then trust their dog's judgment. They will rarely be disappointed.

STEADY TO WING AND SHOT

This phrase refers to training a pointing dog to remain on point until released by the hunter to make a retrieve on a shot bird. It is required for horseback field trial dogs, and for those dogs participating in hunt tests. The advantage to training a dog not to break when the bird flushes is that such a dog will not be in front of the muzzle when the hunter shoots. In a situation where you might be hunting with others who may not be used to hunting with dogs, or whose safety skills are suspect, steady to wing and shot is good way to protect the dog from being accidentally shot. Steady to wing and shot has real safety value in these types of situations.

However, most hunters do not train their dogs to be steady to wing and shot. This is because they want a dog that is moving to retrieve a bird after its flushed. Such a head start puts dogs closer to any birds that come down – increasing their retrieval rates. In addition, such a head start allows dogs to be closer to any birds that might come down crippled. This is particularly important when hunting tough birds such as pheasant or Gambel's quail that can take a lot of shot and still run away from the dog and hunter. With such birds, a matter of seconds can mean the difference between a retrieved bird and one lost in a pack rat midden or tangle of multiflora rose.

My own feeling is that if I were guiding or in a situation that required me to be in hunting situations with my dogs where I didn't know the safe gun handling skills of the other hunters – I would train my dogs to be steady to wing and shot. Otherwise, I think that the increased retrieving effectiveness will continue to keep me training my dogs without steadying them to wing and shot.

13

Safety Afield

When a person brings home their German Shorthair, they make a commitment to care for their dog's welfare and to keep them safe and healthy for the dog's life. That commitment extends to the field. The hazards that a dog and hunter encounter, from barbed wire to rattlesnakes, require that a hunter pay extra attention to the safety of their dog in the field. This is even more important for German Shorthairs because they are tough animals that will continue to hunt with even serious injuries. Every German Shorthair, from the youngest age, must be conditioned to be comfortable with the hunter making regular checks of their body, eyes, and feet – and every hunter should do so regularly in the field.

In addition, every hunter should keep some canine first aid items in their hunting vest, and in a first aid kit at their vehicle. In my vest I typically have: a couple of pairs of hemostats for removing thorns and cactus spines; a leatherman tool with the ability to cut wire; and in a zip lock bag a pair of tweezers for removing fine stickers and grass seeds from eyes, a nail trimmer for dealing with broken toenails; a styptic pencil for small cuts and broken nails, a small tube of triple antibiotic cream, a roll of gauze bandage; glucose tablets; and a tube of EMT gel. Back in my vehicle I also have a first aid kit that includes additional rolls of gauze tape and athletic wrap; compress bandages; adhesive tape; a medical stapler with staples for sealing larger cuts; saline solution in a squeeze bottle for rinsing eyes; Benadryl for allergies and snakebite; enteric aspirin; immodium tablets; antiseptic wipes; hydrogen peroxide for cleaning small cuts and inducing vomiting; a scalpel; veterinary wound spray: wire cutters; and a pair of pliers for removing porcupine quills if the hemostats fail.

The most common canine health incidents that most hunters deal with in the field have to do with small cuts and lacerations, punctures by thorns and quills; and problems with toenails and pads.

CUTS AND LACERATIONS

In the Southwest where I have done so much of my hunting, it sometimes seems that almost everything has the ability to inflict cuts and punctures on my dogs. It is a rare day afield when the dogs don't wind up with some minor cuts on their ears and noses. These often look much worse and more gruesome than they really are. Scratches on the ears often bleed profusely because of the wealth of blood vessels so close to the surface of the skin –and they almost always look much worse than they really are. I once had a Shorthair that had a quarter inch cut on their ear that I had dressed. After the Shorthair had been put in its crate for the drive home, the cut somehow started bleeding again. The dripping tickled the dog, who kept shaking its head in response. When I went to get the dog out of the kennel, it looked as though something had been ax murdered inside it. In the field, such head shaking can cover the neck and even chest of the dog with a veneer of blood that can have you looking in vain for some horrible gash on the neck or body – only to find that the source was a tiny knick on the ear.

Because cuts on the ear tend to bleed more than most – I dress them in the field by rinsing them clean with water to make sure there is no foreign body inside, and then applying a styptic pencil until the bleeding stops. This is typically enough to keep the cut closed. When I get back to the truck I then clean the area with an antiseptic wipe (taking care not to reopen the cut) and then apply antibiotic ointment. Such cuts typically heal in a day or two.

In general most cuts pose little threat to a dog's well being. Unless they are excessively long, excessively deep, or in an area where an artery or ligament might be affected, I typically follow the procedure of keeping them clean, treating them with antibiotic ointment, and monitoring them for infection. With larger cuts I'll also put the dog on a course of antibiotics to prevent complications. Larger cuts that need stitches I typically

Dogs that work in such rugged country will inevitably get cuts and thorns. A hunter needs to know how to treat these.

take to the vet – my wound stapler is for emergencies only. In the beginning it won't do any harm, except to your pocketbook, to err on the side of taking your dog to the vet for treatment when it gets lacerated. As you and your dog gain experience, you will develop some judgment for what you can treat at home, and what your vet should see. However, the rule should always be that when you are in doubt – go to the vet. Better safe than sorry.

THORNS AND PUNCTURES

The vast majority of punctures that your dog will receive will come from thorns or spines on plants. In the southwest, cactus is a common nuisance –and I routinely call my dogs in to check them for cactus spines. I do this not only with my eyes, but with my fingers as well. Cactus spines are hidden by fur, or in between the toes, where they are often not easily obvious –but can be felt with probing fingers. I use hemostats and/or tweezers to remove these spines. Typically, removal is all that is needed for cactus spines or other types of thorns. However, failure to remove spines and thorns can allow them to work their way into the body – perhaps eventually causing serious health problems as they work into vital organs. Foxtails are notorious for this type of burrowing – but other grass seeds, cactus spines, and thorns can do so as well.

One other type of puncture wound that sometimes happens in the field and which can be quite serious is when a running or jumping dog manages to impale themselves on something. Typically this is a branch near or on the ground. Such an occurrence, while rare, usually results in an emergency trip to the nearest vet. If the branch does not break off in the wound, and you are able to see that no organs are punctured, and no veins or arteries damaged, the chances are the dog will be all right with proper care. If the branch is broken off, then you need to make a decision about whether to remove the object. If it is in deep, or if it is near an organ or blood vessel, the best course of action is to immobilize the dog and head to the nearest vet and let them deal with it. Such major puncture wounds require a veterinary examination, cleaning of the wound, and a course of antibiotics.

One final puncture wound worth talking about is the porcupine quill. Where I live porcupines are relatively uncommon – but in many parts of the country the porcupine is a common hazard. For some reason, many dogs that get into porcupines don't seem to learn from the experience. Instead, they seem develop a passionate hatred for porcupines and go out of their way to find and attack them in the field. If I lived in porcupine country, I would put my dog through a course of aversion training with an electronic collar to teach them to avoid porcupines – with particular attention to those dogs who seem to be porcupine haters.

If a dog does get stuck with porcupine quills it is important to get all of the quills out completely. If we are only talking a few quills, you can do this in the field yourself with a pair of pliers or hemostats. When you do pull the quills out, try and put them straight out and put them into a container so that you can look at them later. You want to be able to make sure that no quills broke off, leaving their tips in the dog. This is especially important because porcupine quills are notorious for migrating around a dog's body and causing problems that can eventually result in serious health problems and even death. If you have a dog that got a number of quills on the inside of their mouth and throat – you should take the dog to the vet as soon as possible. These can be very dangerous and typically require putting the dog under anesthesia to get them all.

FOOT INJURIES- PADS AND TOENAILS

Of all of the injuries most regularly incurred by hunting dogs – foot injuries have been the most problematic in my experience. Foot injuries have caused my dogs to miss more days of hunting over the years than all other types of injuries. Of foot injuries, two types are the most prevalent – injuries to the pads, and injuries to toenails.

Where I live, much of the ground over which we hunt is lava rock that is extremely rough on dog's pads. Dog's whose pads soften in the off season generally have problems early in the hunting season. Typically these involve wearing holes in the pad, or tearing a pad. These injuries can be extremely painful to a dog, but fortunately they tend to heal fairly quickly. I tend to treat both types of pad wounds in a similar way – I wash them off with soap and water so that they are clean, then regularly apply antibiotic cream to keep them from getting infected. For tears, if there are ragged edges sticking up that are likely to cause the tear to open even more with use – I'll trim them off with clean manicure scissors. In my experience, it typically takes dogs two or three days to get to the point where they can walk without limping, and about two to three weeks for a dog to be able to hunt again without running the risk of reopening a pad wound.

Toenail injuries are also everyday hazards for a hunting German Shorthair. Typical is the toenail that gets injured on a rock and fractures. A dog's nail consists of a hard covering of longitudinal filaments that cover the "quick" of the nail which is rich in blood vessels and nerve endings. In German Shorthairs, the hard covering of the nail is usually black in color – making it difficult to see how far down the nail the quick ends. On some white dogs with pink pads, the nails may be clear with the quick easily visible. This makes trimming nails much easier than on those with black nails –where determining how much can be trimmed off without hitting the quick is largely educated guesswork.

Injuries to the hard covering of the nail pose little problem in the field - a quick clip with the nail trimmers can usually take care of the problem. It is when damage occurs to the nail that exposes the quick that we have significant problems. Unfortunately, because a dog's nail is made of filaments that run longitudinally along the length of the nail, when a nail breaks it often splinters rather than simply breaking clean. This can expose the quick for much of the length of the nail – which is extremely painful and will bleed to an unpleasant degree. When repairing nail damage what you want to remember is that you want to reconstruct the hard covering of the nail to the extent you can, trim away what you can't, and try to ensure that the rest of the quick is kept away from contact with the air or foreign debris. To do this, you typically will have to stop the bleeding. Wound powder is the method of choice for larger toenail injuries, and a styptic pencil can be used on the rest. In an emergency a mixture of flour and salt can be used as an improvised wound powder. Fortunately, the blood clotted in this method will cover and protect the quick of the nail.

Minor toenail injuries that don't involve significant splintering and which clot successfully can be trimmed up and the dog can often continue hunting after a short rest. I compare this type of injury to the human equivalent of an ingrown toenail. Shattered nails are serious injuries that require an end to field activities and rehabilitation time. Again, the secret is to keep the nail area free of dirt and foreign bodies, keep it covered with antibiotic cream or wound kote, and to trim off any dangling ends that may make the wound worse. Sometimes krazy glue or something similar can be used to glue the nail filaments together again and reform the hard shell –which will make healing easier.

HEAT

Most short haired pointing dogs work best in temperatures from the mid forties to the mid sixties. As temperatures rise over the sixty five degree mark, dogs become progressively more susceptible to heat stroke. So a temperature that is comfortable for humans is actually hot for a hard working German Shorthair. This means we can't just rely on whether we think it's hot - we have to pay special attention to the temperature and the condition of our Shorthairs when we are working them in warm weather.

Dogs are particularly susceptible to heat stroke and cardiac arrest when working in hot weather because the temperature regulating mechanisms of their body are not well designed for operating in hot conditions. The primary means a dog has to regulate body temperature in hot weather is panting. Panting brings blood close to the surface of moist tissue that is cooled by evaporative action, cooling the blood. Blood is also routed into the feet, where perspiration serves to moisten pads and transfer the coolness of the ground to the blood.

In hot weather, these mechanisms are usually efficient enough to keep blood temperatures within the normal range when the dog is at rest in a shady area. However, once the dog starts to exercise, its metabolism generates additional heat as calories are burned - heat which requires additional cooling through panting and heat exchange through the paws. When the amount of internal heat generated exceeds the dog's ability to release it, its core temperature begins to rise, stressing the dog's system. When it rises high enough, the blood actually begins to kill brain cells. If this persists long enough –even just a few minutes - the dog dies.

After more than twenty five years of hunting in Arizona, the following are some rules that have helped me and my German Shorthairs avoid these kind of heat related problems.

♦ *Genetics Matters:* A dogs breed, coat length and color, and genetic makeup largely determine how well it will handle heat.

In German Shorthairs the dogs with more liver or black in their coat have more difficulty with hot weather work. Dark fur passively absorbs solar heat, adding to a darker dog's problems. In the field, my solid liver bitches would always require more rest and feel the heat more than their ticked relatives. The difference wasn't enough to justify not hunting the liver bitches, but it was obvious and enough to have me make sure that they were well watered and monitored for signs of heat stress.

Finally, I believe that some dogs are genetically programmed to handle heat a little better than others. In my experience, lines that have dogs that have suffered from heat stroke in the past seem to produce dogs more likely to get heat stroke themselves. If you have a dog from such lines, take extra care when working in hot conditions.

- *Acclimation is Vital*: Dogs, like humans, are highly adaptable creatures. Given time, a dog's body can adapt, at least partially, to a variety of conditions. Dogs in hotter climates tend to lose insulating layers of fat and develop shorter, thinner coats over time. The more time a dog has to acclimate to hot conditions, the better its body will be equipped to handle the stresses caused by heat.

- *Adjust Your Hunting/Conditioning to Suit the Conditions:* If you are training or hunting during hot weather always try to avoid working your dog during the hottest hours of the day. If you are just conditioning your dog - focus on activities involving water rather than running or road work when the temperature rises above 75. Swimming is great exercise for dogs that like it, and entails far less of a risk of heat stroke.

- *Rest Your Dogs Frequently:* Hunting dogs often push themselves too hard when out in the field on hot days - and don't take enough time to rest and cool down. This is exactly the type of situation that, in hot temperatures, can lead to heat stroke. I normally avoid some of these dangers by insisting that my dogs take a short five to ten minute rest in the shade every 45 minutes or so. The hotter the weather the more frequent the breaks. During these time periods, in addition to assessing how well they are dealing with the heat, I'm able to check my

Shorthairs for thorns, give them water, and wet their head, ears, torso, and feet. If we are hunting near a stock tank, river, or lake, I encourage them to go for a swim.

♦ *Water, Water, Water!* Water is the key element both in preventing heat stroke, and in providing first aid. As a dog pants, it rapidly loses water, much as humans do when they perspire. It needs to regularly replace that water. If this doesn't happen, the dog's natural cooling mechanisms will become progressively less effective until the dog experiences heat exhaustion or heat stroke. It is critical, therefore, to make sure that a dog is watered as often as necessary when working in high temperatures. This may require the dog to consume more than a gallon of water every couple of hours. In the desert, I usually wind up watering my dogs about every twenty minutes, letting them drink until they don't want any more. Often I have to call them in and insist that they stop and drink. I then pour the remaining water on their head and ears - to help in the cooling process.

Water also serves as a heat transfer mechanism - drawing heat out of hot objects and dispersing it. This makes swimming or wading an excellent way to cool a dog down. During the season, I always try and plan my hunts to center around a stock tank or pond. Every hour or so, depending on the temperature, I swing by the pond and let the dogs swim and splash for fifteen minutes or so. This is in addition to the normal rests and water breaks we take. If a swim is not possible, even wading can do some good. A dog's feet and legs have large numbers of arteries and veins close to the surface, and letting a dog stand in cool water for a time can help it to cool down.

Finally, water can also be a life saver. When a dog has begun to show signs of distress from the heat - the most effective first aid treatment is to immerse the dog in a bath of cool water.

♦ *Constantly Monitor Your Dog for Signs of Overheating:* Few dogs just drop from heat exhaustion. Almost all give warning signs of overheating. Every hunter and dog trainer should know those warning signs. The most common ones are as follows:

- Lethargy and sluggishness (dogs that want to rest or refuse to run with their normal vigor and range.)
- Excessive panting
- Bright, blood red gums and tongue (this is a vital warning sign of impending heat stroke, though in some dogs this stage might be too quick to be of value.)
- Staggering, inattentiveness, or drunken type behavior - this is the first stage of heat stroke! A dog exhibiting these symptoms must have it's body temperature lowered as soon as possible!
- Coma - when your dog reaches this stage it's chances of survival are less than fifty percent.

If you see any of these warning signs it is vital that you stop and take action immediately. If the dog is showing signs of overheating, stop and help it to cool down. Take a rest in the shade, give it some water, etc. If it is showing signs of heat stroke, get it into a cool place or bath of cool water as soon as possible, and then get it to a vet. This is an emergency. Heat stroke is deadly serious.

RATTLESNAKES

One of the other hazards that our German Shorthairs face in working in many parts of the American uplands is the potential to come across venomous snakes. Rattlesnakes in particular can pose a serious threat to our dogs. In the late spring and early summer, over much of their range, rattlesnakes emerge from their dens and become more active. This is during training season for many of us. In addition, rattlesnakes will remain active until temperatures drop to the point to push them into hibernation – which can be well into the season in the southern states. While the odds of your dog getting bitten are slim – they are significant enough to merit

RATTLESNAKE!

taking steps to minimize the odds if you are going to be hunting in rattlesnake country.

Rattlesnake bites vary in seriousness. In the worst case scenario, a dog that gets bitten and injected with a full dose of rattlesnake venom can die in less than 30 minutes. Moreover, if treatment with antivenin is required, veterinary bills can run thousands of dollars. However, not every rattlesnake injects a full dose of venom when they bite, and sometimes they won't inject any venom at all. In addition, bites on the head and extremities are often less life threatening because much of the venom remains localized and poses less of a threat to the heart and other vital organs. These bites can still cause severe local tissue damage and can lead to serious infections that can cause death or require amputation. This is why every rattlesnake bite should be treated as a veterinary emergency, and a bitten dog should be brought to a veterinarian as soon as possible.

As with humans, the vast majority of canine snake bites occur because a curious dog pestered or even attacked the snake. Snakes will rarely seek out and attack a dog. With dogs, many, if not most, are bitten on the nose or in the face area precisely because curiosity drew them too close to an angry snake. Teaching dogs to curb that curiosity where rattlesnakes are concerned can literally save their lives. That's what snake avoidance training is designed to do.

Originally developed for hunting dogs in the Southwest who often worked in areas where rattlesnakes are common, snake avoidance training is a specialized type of training that teaches dogs to stay away from rattlesnakes. Trainers, who are also expert snake handlers, remove the fangs from their rattlesnakes before each seminar to ensure that a dog can't get accidentally bit. (This procedure does not harm the snakes, which often break off fangs in the wild and have replacement fangs that will move forward in a few days). The rattlesnake is then placed in an open, accessible area, and the dog is fitted with an electronic collar – and brought over toward the snake. When the dog gets close enough for the snake to strike, the trainer administers a sharp shock to the dog – teaching it that rattlesnakes are something to avoid.

Web Parton, an expert trainer who conducts his "Snake Safe" training clinics around the country, believes that it is important that dogs learn to avoid rattlesnakes by sight, smell, and sound – and so he has developed some special training techniques to teach these things. In addition to introducing the dog to a buzzing rattlesnake in full view, Web also introduces the same dog to rattlesnakes that have had their tail taped are unable to buzz, and rattlesnakes that are placed in a mesh bag and therefore hidden from sight. He believes that once dogs have learned to avoid the sight, sound, and smell of rattlesnakes, they have the best protection that training can give.

Web also cited an important additional benefit to having your dog trained to avoid rattlesnakes. "Certainly we train dogs to avoid snakes in order to protect the dog. However, an important added benefit for the people with a dog that has been "snake safe" trained is that the dog can serve as an early warning system to let them know that a snake is there. Dogs have an amazing sense of smell. We focus on the scent component of the training to be sure that the dog can pick up the snake at a distance – and by its avoidance behavior alert people to the presence of a snake they too can then avoid."

A full snake breaking session for a dog takes about a half hour and usually costs anywhere from $65 to $90 depending upon the trainer. In addition, many Animal shelters and dog clubs offer snake breaking seminars to their members at a reduced cost. Professional trainers such as Web Parton also conduct snake breaking clinics around the country. For more information on snake avoidance training and upcoming snake breaking clinics you can check the snakesafe.com section of Web Parton's website at <u>http://birddoguniversity.com/</u>, or you can contact hunting dog trainers in your area.

14

Breeding Your German Shorthair

Anyone that owns a decent female German Shorthair will, at some time, ponder the question of whether or not to breed her. If the inclination is beginning to go beyond the pondering state, there are some things that you should know before you take the plunge.

The first thing to recognize is that the animal shelters are filled with unwanted dogs – too many of them German Shorthairs. The world has no need for more litters of badly bred German Shorthair puppies. So unless you are willing to devote the time and effort necessary to breeding superior pups - you are better off not starting at all. Get the bitch spayed.

Breeding German Shorthairs is an undertaking that is equal parts science and art. A responsible breeder must have a basic grounding in the science of genetics, as well as a keen eye and gift for assessing and matching up breeding stock. If you are willing to put in the time to do the homework, then here is an overview of what you need to know.

STARTING OUT

Every good litter and line starts with a good brood bitch. Most experienced breeders will tell you that the bitch is the most important part of the mix. In golf they say you drive for show but you putt for dough. In breeding the sire's for show, the dam's for dough. However, not every female German Shorthair makes a good brood bitch. The hallmark of a good breeder is the ability to make a ruthlessly realistic assessment of a bitch to determine whether she should be bred at all.

To do this requires some time. Only outstanding German Shorthair bitches should be bred. In this regard, pedigree is no substitute for performance. To know whether a bitch is outstanding takes at least two or three seasons in the field. Many bitches have come on during their first year like they were going to be in the hall of fame, only to backslide during their sophomore year and turn out to be mediocre at best.

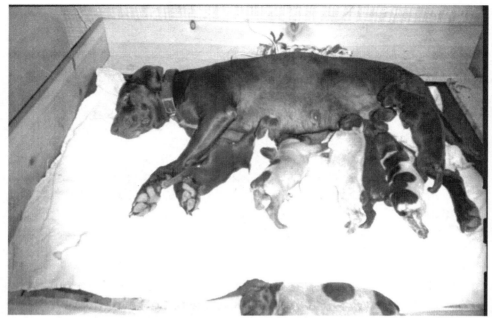
Anyone that owns a decent female German Shorthair will, at some time, ponder the question of whether or not to breed her.

Waiting until your bitch is at least two before breeding gives you a chance to make a reasonable assessment of her strengths and weaknesses. These strengths and weaknesses are the expressed characteristics of her genes – the genes she will pass to her pups. If she passes the assessment, if she's worth breeding, then the fun begins.

GENETICS (YIKES!)

Genes are collections of molecules and other goodies that link together to form DNA, the building blocks of life. It is DNA lined up on chromosomes that organizes protoplasm and gunk into Playboy centerfolds or German Shorthairs (pretty amazing, huh!), and genes are the instructions on the DNA about what goes where and does what. There are a few things that are important for the novice breeder to know about genes.

- Genes are " the functional and physical unit of heredity passed from parent to offspring."
- Genes are always found in pairs on chromosomes (VERY IMPORTANT).

214

- Genes are dominant or recessive. A dominant gene will always override its pair partner to express a characteristic, but a recessive gene must be paired with another recessive gene to express its characteristic.
- Genes are often linked –so the gene for black hair is always associated with the gene for a black nose in a purebred Labrador for example. Genes are also often interactive, working together in combination to produce expressed characteristics.
- A dog (or human) gets one half of its genes from its sire, and one half from its dam which are combined in the chromosomes of each new fetus. How these genes pair determines what characteristics the dog will have.

As noted above, genes occur in pairs – one coming from each parent. When different genes (dominant+recessive) pair together they are known as heterozygous genes. When two genes of the same type (dominant+dominant and recessive+recessive) pair together they are known as homozygous genes. Two parents with identical sets of homozygous genes will produce pups with genes identical to themselves.

Inbreeding (mating two directly related dogs), or close line breeding (mating two dogs related within two generations), decreases genetic variation and increases homozygosity – which increases consistency among a litter. The more pups are genetically like their parents, the more likely they are also to be like them in appearance, temperament, ability, etc. This is an attractive quality for big breeders turning out lots of pups – they can be sure of the qualities and characteristics of their pups.

However, increased homozygosity also increases the likelihood for expressed genetic maladies in a litter and line. Most genetic abnormalities and diseases occur on recessive genes. They are not normally expressed in a heterozygous gene pair because the dominant gene cancels them out. All dogs have a great number of these pairs of bad recessive genes masked by good dominant genes. When you increase homozygosity, you increase the likelihood that these recessive genes will pair up – and the pups will wind up with undescended testicles, hip dysplasia, incorrect bites, hypoglycemia, epilepsy, etc. This is why inbreeding and close line breeding is best left to the experts that are so inclined.

There is a complicated mathematical formula to measure homozygosity called the coefficient of inbreeding (COI). This formula is available on some veterinary websites. Many breeders use the COI to help them keep that balance of desirable homozygosity and genetic variety.

TAKING STOCK

Assessing the strengths and weaknesses of breeding stock is much of what makes breeding an art rather than a science. It requires a keen eye, and an ability to detach oneself from any emotional baggage about an animal and to make an impartial assessment of a dog. It's what makes the great breeders great.

I always advise a novice breeder to use a Zen approach to this aspect of breeding. Close your eyes and envision the perfect hunting dog for the type of hunting you do. How does she move and range? What type of temperament does she have? How does she handle? What type of build and coat does she have? Does she have good conformation within the breed standards? Assemble a mental checklist of those qualities typically affected by heredity that this ideal dog possesses. . The qualities I tend to focus on are (not in any specific order) as follows:

- Natural Pointing and Retrieving Ability
- Nose
- Range
- Conformation
- Temperament
- Bidability
- Intelligence
- Drive

Now open your eyes and look at your bitch and make a comparison to that ideal dog. How does your bitch measure up? Assign a number from one to ten to each of the qualities you identified, and be brutally honest. Once you've rated your bitch this way, you'll have a good idea of her strengths and weaknesses, and where you need to go in your breeding. If she scored well on the checklist, then you are set to take the next step.

The next step is getting a medical assessment of her health. Waiting until your bitch is two gives you the opportunity to have her hips x-rayed for OFA or Penn Hip certification. Hip dysplasia is a relatively common genetic disorder that can be identified through a special review of hip x-rays. For breeds with known problems with HD, all breeding stock should be certified HD free before breeding. Depending upon the breed, screening for a variety of other genetic disorders might be recommended. She should also be tested for brucellosis. It is best to discuss with your vet what tests might be appropriate for your breed.

Now that you have determined that you have a bitch that performs well in the field, has good conformation within breed standards, is medically sound, and has the personality characteristics you would want in your pups - the next step is to find a stud.

CHOOSING A STUD

Picking the stud is where most amateur breeders fail. Too often they pick a stud that is convenient, or one that is famous, without assessing whether the stud will adequately compliment the bitch. The net result of such pairings is nothing more than a gamble - sometimes it works and often it doesn't.

When we were assessing the bitch, we developed a mental image of the ideal hunting dog. Ideally, we want our pups to fit this description. We want to breed pups better than their parents. As we have already assessed the strengths and weaknesses of our dam, we need to figure what characteristics we need in a stud to get us from her to our ideal pups. Surveying our checklist for the bitch should give us some idea of the characteristics we want in the stud. You might want to make a checklist for the stud as well, and then see if you can find a dog to match.

If our bitch already fits our profile of a perfect dog, and we want to ensure that the pups are as similar to her as possible, we should consider close line breeding or inbreeding. By such close breeding we diminish the genetic variation and increase homozygosity, heightening our chances of getting pups that are very close in appearance and behavior to their parents. On the other hand, we also increase the potential for genetic maladies such as inbreeding depression, hypoglycemia, etc. These risks have to be weighed against the benefits.

Assuming that the bitch is not perfect, and has some weaknesses we would want to see improved in the pups - then we need to find a stud that can do the job. The key to remember is that when you breed, genes don't mix like liquor in a martini. The pups will be a combination of the genes of their mother and father, not a mix. In a Martini, if you have too much vermouth you can add more gin to balance things out. With dogs, if you have a big running bitch and you want a more moderate range in the pups, you can't breed to a boot polisher and assume it will wash out. What you will likely get is a litter in which half are big runners and half are boot polishers. You have to aim for what you want – not the opposite of your dam.

Finally, you have to make sure that the stud is healthy as well. He should be tested for brucellosis as well as any potential genetic problems.

Once you've got a stud that you believe has the characteristics you want, you need to take a look at the pedigree and genetic background of both dogs to try and determine if they share enough genes to ensure that he might make a good genetic match for your bitch.

ASSESSING A PEDIGREE

The fundamental reason for the existence of canine breed registries is to provide an accurate pedigree. A pedigree is a record of the genetic inheritance of a dog. As such, it can be extremely valuable in making breeding decisions. Typical pedigrees contain a record of the ancestry of a dog - generally out to five generations. A good pedigree will list the registered name of each dog, and any credentials and titles it might have gained. Some typical abbreviations that you will see in a hunting dog pedigree include FC (Field Champion AKC), CH (Field Champion FDSB/Bench Champion AKC), DC (Dual champion –a champ in both field and show), MH, SH, JH (Master, Senior, and Junior Hunter).

One word of caution about field trial titles. There are different types of field trial formats, and a dog requires different characteristics to win in these formats. If you are trying to tone down the range of your bitch, you certainly don't want to breed to a line of All Age field trial champions. FC or CH tells you the dog had the right stuff to win in its format. It doesn't tell you in which format a dog competed for its championship. Nor does it tell you the characteristics needed to win in that format. It's up to you to find out these important facts. Also, don't be put off of a great dog that doesn't have many FCs in it's pedigree. Many fine hunting dogs have no FC or CH in front of their names simply because their owners didn't have the inclination or money to compete in field trials.

When comparing two pedigrees to determine breeding suitability you want to look for common ancestors – hopefully with some titles. These are genetic intersection points – genes that both dogs will have in common and will pass on to the pups. The closer these intersection points are to the proposed pup, the more shared genes it will have. The more shared genes, the more likely a pup is to "throw true," (resemble in conformation, temperament, and ability it's parents). However, the more genes the parents have in common, the greater potential for reproductive problems, and that the pups will exhibit genetic maladies (more about this in the genetics section). Therefore, most breeders try and balance the desire for a common genetic foundation to ensure that the pups will throw true, against the dangers of too much inbreeding. In my own case, I try and look for three or four intersection points (common ancestors) between the third and fifth generation, and if these intersection points are DCs, things get better and better!!

MECHANICS

Normally if you put a healthy female in heat down with a healthy male – nature will take its course. This is true of the vast majority of breedings. However, there are times when things don't go quite as planned. Sometimes this is a human mistake, sometimes a canine problem, and sometimes it's just an act of God.

The most common human mistake is to put the pair together too soon. Canine estrus has three phases. They are slightly different for each bitch. The first phase, pre-estrus – is characterized by bloody spotting and swelling of the vulva. It usually lasts about a week. During this period a bitch can not conceive, and won't accept the male. The second period is estrus – the time when the bitch is fertile and can conceive. This is characterized by watermelon colored or clear liquid coming from the vulva, and she will stand and move her tail to one side when you put your hand upon her hips. Estrus normally lasts about a week. The final period is anestrus – in which the bitch moves out of heat if she has not conceived. Traditionally, dogs are put together about ten days after the first spotting is sighted, and again 12 days after. A veterinarian can do hormone tests to tell you exactly when the bitch is in estrus if you have doubts about your own ability to tell.

The most common canine mistakes are caused by inexperience and nervousness. Sometimes a young male, though willing, won't have the mechanics worked out quite right and may need help to hit the bull's-eye. Other times a bitch may be nervous, or may not find the male attractive, and will refuse to stand. At such times the owner holding the bitch's head can prevent the male from receiving some potentially dangerous bites. Generally, a rule of thumb is to bring the bitch to the male so she will feel less dominant outside of her own territory, while he will feel more assertive in his own territory. Finally, if the bitch is still nervous after the tie (dogs remain connected for up to a half hour) it may be necessary to hold her or tie her up. An agitated bitch can seriously injure a male during the tie.

Finally, there are times when two willing dogs can't seem to tie – or even after a successful tie the bitch doesn't conceive. Often these are health related problems, and a trip to the vet can clear up the mystery. Sometimes these problems can be solved – sometimes they can't.

CONCLUSION

Once you pick the stud and dam – and roll the dice – you won't really know if you've been successful for at least a year or two. That's when you can get feedback from those that bought your pups. If you've hit a homer with the litter, the feeling of pride and accomplishment will more than cover for the hard work and time that you put into creating the litter.

15

Odds and Ends

There are some aspects of life with German Shorthairs that don't fit into nicely defined categories – but merit at least some comment. Many of them have to do with German Shorthair idiosyncrasies and, if you have a sense of humor, add to the breed's charm.

One of the aspects of living with a German Shorthair that is both a blessing and a pain is the breed's intelligence. German Shorthairs are smart – at times scary smart. When this intelligence is turned toward finding birds and helping people – it is a blessing. When this formidable intelligence is turned toward getting out of confinement, getting at forbidden food, or breaking house rules – German Shorthairs can be frustrating pains in the butt. Fortunately, if you retain the ability to laugh at misfortune – many of these incidents can be quite comical.

A good example of this is what I call:

The Great Macaroni and Cheese Incident

A few years back Charlie, a good friend, volunteered to house sit and mind the dogs while I went out of town on a business trip. Charlie was a confirmed lab man - and my German Shorthaired Pointers were the first real introduction he'd had to the breed.

At first he was a little leery of these dogs "with no hair and no tails," but some time spent chasing quail with Annchen and her pups Rosie and Billy helped them all forge a friendly bond. One of the things he quickly discovered is that my German Shorthairs are smart as whips, and you have to be on your toes when you are around them.

The other thing he discovered is that they could communicate very clearly. Now I won't say that they can talk, exactly - but they can come pretty darn close. When Charlie missed three easy singles in a row - there was no mistaking what Annchen, the old matriarch of the family said to him. "The sun was in my eyes," Charley replied to her with some heat, "and anyway, there's no way you could shoot better than I can - you don't even have any thumbs!" Annchen gave him a final disgusted look and moved on.

As we followed, I commiserated. "Don't feel bad. A few years ago I had a shooting slump that lasted four weeks. At the end of that time, she wouldn't even talk to me. She would give me the cold shoulder all the way home and for days afterward. If I hadn't gotten over that slump when I did, I'm pretty sure she was planning on filing for divorce."

Eventually, Charlie got the hang of hitting our desert quail, and Annchen and the pups warmed up to him pretty well. They got to be good buddies. So when I got word that I had to travel to New York City on business for a week, and I was telling him about how I hated to board them at the vet's for that long a time, Charlie volunteered to stay at my place and watch the dogs for the week. The payback was that I had to watch his lab, Jenny, when he went back home to South Dakota to visit his parents a few weeks later. It seemed like an all around good deal for everyone concerned.

Before I left, I warned Charlie to leave the dogs out in the backyard during the daytime when he went to work. After bitter experience with generations of von Geldie GSPs my back yard had evolved into the equivalent of a canine maximum security yard - with an electric wire to discourage tunneling running along the bottom of a six foot wooden fence. Despite these formidable precautions, the back yard itself was actually a large canine playground. All pretense at planting flowers or shrubbery had long since been abandoned. Now it was just a large grass expanse filled with dog toys, excavations, and flat roofed dog houses that everyone preferred to rest on rather than in. The dogs were perfectly happy to spend a workday in the back yard roughhousing with each other, chewing on bones, or stalking the various sparrows and pigeons that flew in to pick grit and prospect for seeds.

I flew off on my business trip confident that Charlie, an old dog hand, would take care of Annchen, Billy, and Rosie like they were his own - and that everyone would have a fun week. I was a little surprised, when I got home a week later and Charlie met me at the door with the words "I cleaned

224

everything up as best I could - but there was cheese everyplace."

As I said hello to three German Shorthairs that were ecstatic to see me again -and one lab that was pretty happy as well - I rapidly checked to make sure that everyone had all of their limbs and eyes. All the dogs appeared fine - so I asked Charlie what he was talking about.

Charlie said, "Everything was fine all week long. I left the dogs in the backyard as you suggested, and I took Jenny in to work with me as I normally do. Yesterday it looked like it was going to rain, so I decided to leave your dogs in the house. They had been well behaved angels all week, and I didn't think there would be any trouble. I made sure to put everything that a dog might get into up on counters or otherwise out of their reach - so I was confident that everything would be ok."

"I knew that something was wrong when I didn't hear the dogs barking and whining when I pulled in that evening. I was a little worried that something had happened. I opened the door, and your entire living room was yellow -and I mean yellow!! Even the bed in your bedroom was yellow - and there was macaroni scattered everywhere. The dogs had somehow opened one of the cabinets and gotten out a six pack of those dry Macaroni and Cheese Dinners and had shredded them. They must have played tug of war and keep away with the boxes - because I even found macaroni on the top of the tall bookcases and behind the couch.

Annchen and Billy had gone to their beds in the bedroom and came out yawning sleepily - trying to pretend that they had been asleep and hadn't realized any of this happened. They knew I wasn't buying any of it - and their courage was failing. That's when Rosie tried another tack." (Rosie at that time was a one year old, solid liver female that looked like a little angel - but was the most mischievous hellion I'd ever had. Her stunning beauty and soft eyes had saved her many a sore behind.)

"Rosie began telling me about how some burglars had broken in to the house and attempted to steal the Macaroni and Cheese dinners, but how she bravely fought them and eventually drove them off. This story would have been more believable if her face hadn't literally been covered with yellow dried cheese powder. As horrible as it was - I couldn't help laughing. I've never seen a dog try such a brazen, bald faced lie. I sent them all to their crates, and spent most of last night trying to clean up. It was a major mess. I think you've still got cheese powder inside the TV."

I couldn't help but laugh, and Charley looked relieved. "I think that 'may you have smart dogs,' is an ancient Chinese curse - and nobody knows their curses like those ancient Chinese," I said. "As long as nobody was hurt, and nothing was broken - I think I got off pretty lightly." Even though the living room had the faint aroma of cheese for months afterward - I think I did get off pretty lightly. I've known smart dogs that broke up marriages and got folks evicted.

As Charlie was leaving, he turned and said, "you know, I'm convinced that it was Rosie that did it, but I can't figure out how she opened the cabinet. It has those spring clips to keep toddlers from opening it." I replied, "I'd bet you're right. Rosie is the troublemaker of the family - though none of them are up for sainthood. As for how she figured it out - well if dogs could take IQ tests I bet she'd score higher than anyone in the state legislature."

Charley laughed as he got into his truck, "there's nothing worse than having three smart dogs cooped up and bored for a day, is there?." I just smiled. Actually, there is - having four smart dogs cooped up and bored for a day. That reminds me of what happened when I looked after Jenny - but that's a story for another time.

Top 10 Favorite Shorthair Tricks

With regular dog breeds, this section would normally be interpreted as the kinds of tricks you can teach your Shorthair to perform. With German Shorthairs it refers to those classic tricks that Shorthairs like to pull on us. I think that this propensity for practical jokes is genetic with German Shorthairs, because they all pull them. You just have to learn to be on your guard.

1. *The Snootfull*: It is amazing how much water the jowls of a German Shorthair will hold. Perhaps the favorite

Shorthair trick is to get a snootfull of water from the dish (or even better the toilet) and then come, under the guise of seeking affection, to deposit it on your clothes. Shorthairs get extra points if they manage to do this on your best clothing such as business suits, silk dresses and ties, gowns, etc. minutes before you are due at some public function.

2. *The Head Butt*: There may be natural substances harder than the top of a German Shorthairs head, but after you've received a head butt you'll be hard pressed to think of what they might be. Typically this occurs when you are bending down to give your dog affection. Your Shorthair will then quickly look up, head butting you in the jaw or nose. My father lost a tooth from a particularly good head butt, and I've had a couple of bloody noses and countless pairs of glasses damaged from Shorthair head butts over the years. Use caution when bending down with your head over your Shorthair's – it could be a trap.

3. *The Stare*: When a German Shorthair wants' attention there's a variety of ways they seek it. The stare is a favorite. This typically occurs after you have told your Shorthair to go away because you are too busy at that moment to heed their wishes. The dog will then locate itself where you can easily see it, and stare. It's like being spotlighted in a pair of headlights. This usually occurs as you are experiencing a romantic moment, watching the climax of a sporting event or movie, or are carrying on a conversation on the telephone. A squirt bottle filled with water is a good counter to this.

4. *The Punch*: If the stare doesn't work, Shorthairs will often resort to the punch. This is particularly true of a dog trying to get you to throw the tennis ball or bumper it has in its mouth. This consists of using a single front paw to swipe at you to get your attention. Unfortunately for men, given the Shorthair's size, this often results in a punch delivered in the groin area – which can be remarkably painful if you are caught unaware. Always beware of a Shorthair sitting near you with a ball in its mouth.

5. *The Surreptitious Sample*: German Shorthairs are attracted to human food and drink – almost as much as Labradors are. This makes any human food or drink on a coffee table or end table a severe temptation – and Shorthairs don't believe in resisting temptation. They just believe in not getting caught. This means that at a dinner party or gathering – any food or drink that is not under constant observation is fair game for a taste. Shorthair tongues often wind up in glasses of wine, beer, hors d'oeuvres, appetizer plates – and unguarded sandwiches, bits of cheese, etc. often wind up pilfered and devoured in a distant corner. The best defense is to not allow a Shorthair to "mingle" at a dinner party or gathering – and to limit the amount of forage available at Shorthair height.

6. *The Major Heist*: Not every German Shorthair has the nerve to pull this one off – but all of them think about it. This trick usually occurs around a special occasion such as a holiday or gathering – where special foods are left on the counter or table. The Thanksgiving turkey, Christmas cookies, Sunday roast, Valentines chocolates – are like world class diamonds to a famous jewel thief where Shorthairs are concerned. If they have the opportunity and the ability – there's a good chance that Thanksgiving may wind up sans Turkey. Joking aside, this can actually be deadly dangerous to a German Shorthair where chocolate is concerned – so all chocolate needs to be kept well away from potential Shorthair theft. The obvious solution to the big heist is to keep a good guard over the kitchen, and to keep Shorthairs and holiday food separate. I typically keep the Shorthairs outside during major cooking sessions, or forbid them entry into the kitchen/dining area (even if this requires crating).

7. *The Big Stink*: One of the obvious ways we know that a dog's sense of smell is different from our own is that they seem to find particularly attractive those smells that we find nauseating. Some Shorthairs love to anoint themselves with particularly malodorous materials – animal and human feces; the putrefying remains of long dead animals, sewage and various effluents, etc. They will roll and roll in such

materials – and then come to you to share the fun. Usually, they will try and get some loving so that they can wipe some of the stuff on you and your clothes. I've actually had to burn some of the clothes that my Shorthairs have managed to infuse with particularly nauseating odors. At the very least, I've reached down to pet my beloved Shorthair – only to have my hand come up covered with feces. The only remedy for this trick is to keep aware of the location of dogs that like to pull it, to keep them away from you and anything that could get "the stink" until the dog can be washed, and to make sure that you have a non-leaking plastic crate in which to haul them home for a bath if you need to.

8. *The Napkin*: This is an interesting variation of the snootful. Being of noble birth, German Shorthairs typically have elegant table manners. After scarfing down whatever it is that they are eating – they will then thoroughly clean the remnants off of their chin and jowls. They do this by wiping their chin and jowels off on various napkin substitutes: the rug (the lighter colored and more expensive the better), your good clothes, the baby, your sleeping bag, or whatever else might come to hand. As with the snootful, this is sometimes masked by a plea for affection. Often you will pleasantly stroke the ears of your German Shorthair as they rest their head on your lap, only to find that when they depart they have left a nice food print on your clothes. The best solution to the napkin is to wipe off the chins and jowls of German Shorthairs after they have eaten.

9. *The Misdirection*: This one has a number of variations. The basis of the misdirection is that your dog will give some sort of false alert to divert your attention so that they are then able to achieve an objective they want. This one is most often pulled on other dogs in the house, but is used on humans as well. Classic examples include the dog that barks at the door leading you to get up and see what's outside only to find that in the meantime your German Shorthair has stolen your seat. Another classic is the German Shorthair that locks up into false points as you get

close to the truck at the end of the day – forcing you to prolong your time afield.

10. *The Houdini*: German Shorthairs have justly earned a reputation as talented escape artists. What they can't tunnel under, they pry apart, unravel, lever open, or simply bust through. In my back yard I strung a low voltage electric livestock wire along the bottom of my wooden fence to discourage my German Shorthairs from tunneling out – something that was happening routinely before the wire put an end to it. I've seen German Shorthairs run completely through the screen on a screen door to get at a cat in the front yard. I've also seen German Shorthairs that could open the same screen door using the handle, and ones that could turn doorknobs. Others have unraveled the wire on a chain link fence, and have learned to operate the latches on the gates to their kennels. The only advice I can give about such dogs is to take appropriate countermeasures as needed – and not to underestimate the escape abilities of your German Shorthair.

INDEX

Dr. Jim Reiser (Shooting Starr Kennels), 31

Dual Champions, 32, 70, 219

Electronic collar, 140, 146, 169, 170, 182, 202, 210

Epilepsy, 27, 68, 216

Ernst Rojem, 31

Estrus, 220

Farming, 12

Feeding, 27, 85, 95, 96, 109, 161, 193

FEMALE, GSP CHARACTERISTICS, 72

Fetch, retrieving command, 129, 131, 150, 153

Field Dog Stud Book – American registry, 16, 29, 80, 81, 82, 83, 219

Field trial participants, 4, 6, 9, 15, 17, 18, 60, 61, 79, 80, 81, 99, 180, 182, 197

Field trial strains of German shorthairs, 15, 17, 70, 79, 100

Field trial style German Shorthairs, 15

FIELD TRIALS AND HUNTING GSPs, 80

Field Trials, all age, 62, 65, 81, 82, 83, 99, 219

Field Trials, gun dog, vii, 82, 125, 126

Field Trials, shooting dog, 82

Field Trials, walking stakes, 83

Finding a breeder, 66, 85, 91, 92, 111

First aid kit, components of, 199

First aid, cuts and lacerations, 74, 119, 199, 200

First aid, puncture wounds, 202

First aid, styptic pencil, 75, 199, 200, 204

First aid, thorns and punctures, 39, 59, 74, 199, 200, 201, 207

First aid, toenail injuries, 44, 199, 203, 204

FIRST DAY, BRINGING A PUP HOME, 89, 191

Foot injuries, 203

Force, 9, 101, 102, 119, 121, 126, 132, 140, 161, 166, 170, 171, 196

Form vs. Function, 35

French pointers (Braques), 23, 24, 25

Frostbite, 40

Gastric torsion (bloat), 96

Gastric torsion, (bloat), 96

Genes, 27, 33, 37, 57, 58, 59, 61, 64, 67, 68, 69, 104, 125, 126, 162, 179, 205, 213, 214, 215, 216, 217, 218, 219, 226

Genes, dominant, 215

Genes, recessive, 69, 215

Georgia, 32

German Hunter, 11

Give command, 5, 7, 30, 39, 54, 79, 85, 87, 92, 93, 94, 95, 97, 98, 99, 111, 114, 115, 116, 118, 119, 120, 121, 122, 124, 126, 129, 130, 131, 133, 134, 140, 141, 144, 145, 147, 148, 151, 153, 154, 156, 166, 173, 175, 179, 185, 187, 194, 207, 208, 210, 217, 224, 227, 229, 230

Golden thread, 190

Gun, introduction to, 161

Gunshyness, 161, 162, 164

Habitat, 12

Lightning Source UK Ltd.
Milton Keynes UK

177092UK00001B/49/P